GROUND

M50/M50A1 Ontos

Self-Propelled Multiple 106 mm Recoilless Rifle

DAVID DOYLE

Library of Congress Control Number: 2022932594

Cover design by Justin Watkinson
Type set in Impact/Minion Pro/Univers LT Std

ISBN: 978-0-7643-6512-6
Printed in China

Published by Schiffer Publishing, Ltd.
4880 Lower Valley Road
Atglen, PA 19310
Phone: (610) 593-1777; Fax: (610) 593-2002
Email: Info@schifferbooks.com
Web: www.schifferbooks.com

Acknowledgments

This book would not have been possible without the generous help of the late Don Moriarty, who was one the leading experts on the Ontos. Don generously shared his knowledge of the Ontos as well as volunteered to photograph the vehicle he so painstakingly restored for the Patton Museum. Also instrumental in the creation of this book were my friends Tom Kailbourn, Scott Taylor, the late Dave Harper, and the staff of the former Patton Museum, as well as the La Porte County Historical Society, the Naval History and Heritage Command, the TACOM LCMC History Office, the USMC, and the Ordnance Museum. Special thanks go to my darling wife, Denise, who stood firmly by me as I labored on this long into the nights.

Contents

Introduction

As the US Army considered new equipment following World War II, increased emphasis was placed on fielding air mobile equipment, as well as equipment that had increased ground mobility as compared to what was then in the field. The rapid outbreak of the war in Korea and the initial devastating losses by United Nations forces convinced the US Army that there was an urgent requirement for an inexpensive, rapidly deployable armored vehicle to transport, which could be fitted with a recoilless rifle for antitank use.

The Infantry Fighter

Secretary of the Army Frank Pace and the Army chief of staff, Gen. J. Lawton Collins, expressed great interest in this concept, spurring rapid development.

In February 1951, the chief of ordnance asked Detroit Arsenal to consider a vehicle proposed by Maj. Gen. Rex Webb Beasley, chief of staff, Research & Development Section, Office of the Chief of Army Field Forces.

On March 8, 1951, Detroit Arsenal staff met with representatives of Allis-Chalmers, Ford, and General Motors to discuss the requirements for the new series of vehicles. During this meeting, Carl Rasmussen (chief, Combat Vehicles Branch) and engineer LeRoy Reinke presented the initial design of the "Infantry Fighter Vehicle" as put together by Detroit Arsenal.

By the end of April 1951, the decision had been made that the vehicle would be armed with four 105 mm recoilless rifles. On June 21, 1951, it was decided that the vehicle would be powered by the six-cylinder GMC 302-cubic-inch gasoline truck engine, then being used in the M135/M211-series 2½-ton 6 × 6 trucks. The engine would be coupled to an Allison XT-90 cross-drive transmission, and the armament increased to six 105 mm recoilless rifles. Development of the vehicle was given the security classification "Confidential"—the lowest of the Army's rankings.

By August 1951, word about the new vehicle, known variously as "the Infantry Fighter" or "the Infantry Gun Vehicle," reached a study group in California working on top-secret projects.

Project Vista

In the years immediately following World War II, there was considerable concern in the US about the spread of communism and the increase in weaponry of the already-powerful Soviet military, and the growing military of Communist China. When war broke out in Korea, the rapid advance of Communist forces raised great concern in the US military, and those concerns led to careful study. In the fall of 1950, California Institute of Technology (Caltech) nuclear physicist Charles Lauritsen was among those touring Korean battlefields, and Lauritsen noted that US ground forces needed better-coordinated tactical air support. He brought this need to the attention of Caltech's trustees upon his return stateside. He advocated that Caltech take on a study to address the threat of a Soviet invasion of Europe. Ultimately, a contract was awarded in an amount approaching three-quarters of a million dollars, which would involve about a quarter of Caltech's full-time faculty members. The objective of the study was to determine the most-effective ways that weapons already in use could be employed to counter a Soviet advance in Europe.

The Caltech study group, which grew to include 120 participants, including thirty-nine Caltech faculty and fifteen from Cornell, became known as Project Vista, taking its name from the government building that housed its offices, the former Vista del Arroyo hotel in Pasadena. Classified as top secret, Project Vista was undertaken from April 2, 1951, through December 1 of the same year, producing—through

8,500 man-hours of work by thirteen special study groups—a report containing numerous recommendations for each of the armed services.

The Vista report, much of which remains classified to this day, was not well received by the Air Force, which felt that its emphasis on tactical weapons undermined that service's "Strategic Deterrence" approach. The Army, on the other hand, while not embracing all 260 Army-related recommendations in the report, did find much of it favorable.

The Vista Project advocated defensive equipment rather than offensive equipment, which drew the ire of some in the Pentagon. This was not lost on the Vista writers, who wrote (and the Pentagon seemingly ignored, in large part), "In the past has been the United States military emphasis on offensive capability. As we look back upon wars in which we have enjoyed ultimate success, we find, not unnaturally, that victory came as the result of offensive, not defensive, action. The present organization, and present military thinking, is therefore strongly slanted toward offensive action. Acknowledging the fact that we will not start the next war and that we will inevitably be less prepared for it than the aggressor, it follows that the initial action will be defensive on our part and our present organization my not be appropriate."

In line with the above, the Vista Project scientists and military advisors advocated that there should be developed and fielded thousands of small, agile antitank vehicles, each armed with multiple recoilless rifles, as the primary practical way to counter a massed Soviet armored assault. The Vista writers dubbed this proposed, somewhat nebulous vehicle defensive vehicle as "ONTOS" and wrote, "A highly mobile anti-tank vehicle such as the ONTOS appears to represent the most rapid means of producing a strong anti-tank capability."

Counter to what many have postulated for decades, "Ontos" is Greek for "indeed," rather than "the thing." However, it does seem likely that when others read the Vista Project report, those readers would have substituted "the thing" for the hypothetical ONTOS called for by the writers of the report.

The Vista Project's ONTOS and Ordnance's "the Infantry Fighter" shared many common characteristics, so it not surprising that that Ontos moniker was applied to the Ordnance vehicle. The Vista scientists wrote, "Our requirements for 6,636 Ontos antitank vehicles, six million conventional antitank mines, and fourteen million unremovable antitank mines is within the capacity of NATO to supply on position within a relatively short time."

CHAPTER 1

Ontos Is Born

A T55 tracked utility vehicle, which shared the same chassis as the Ontos and a similar superstructure, is on the ramp of a USAF Douglas C-124 Globemaster II transport aircraft. The tapering form of the superstructure limited the vehicle's capacity and, consequently, its utility. Ventilation louvers for the engine compartment were on the front part of the right side of the superstructure. *TACOM LCMC History Office*

On September 22, 1951, the chief of Army Field Forces, Gen. Mark W. Clark, wired the deputy chief of staff with his list of proposed pilot vehicles for the program. The deputy chief of staff then ordered that Ordnance move ahead with development of the Ontos. Two weeks later, on October 6, Army secretary Pace directed Gen. Collins to assign the project the highest priority and to provide the secretary with semimonthly project reports. According to congressional testimony, "Development was initiated on October 11, 1951."

After having considered design proposals from Ford, General Motors, and Allis-Chalmers, on October 26, 1951, Allis-Chalmers Manufacturing Co. was awarded a letter contract to produce twelve pilot vehicles and two further kits. Allis-Chalmers Manufacturing Company, best known for its farm equipment, was in fact a very large, heavy American industrial firm with considerable engineering talent at its disposal. The breakdown of the order was as follows:

(1) two vehicles, T55 (six-man personal carrier)
(2) two vehicles, T56 (ten-man personnel carrier)
(3) two T164 kits (four-rifle turret)
(4) four vehicles, T165 (six rifles)
(5) two vehicles, T166 (one rifle)
(6) two vehicles, T167 (eight rifles)

The letter award was in the amount of $1,218,998. The letter contract allowing the Tractor Division of Allis-Chalmers to begin work, which was assigned a 1A priority rating, was done in earnest, while the final specifications, terms, and price were still being negotiated.

It would be April 1952 before the final, definitive fixed-price contract was awarded. That contract carried a $2,448,200 price tag.

Within two weeks of the initial signing, Allis-Chalmers, at times involving fifty engineers, had completed the design of the M50. Due to the "Confidential" classification of this project by the military, a portion of Allis-Chalmers' La Porte, Indiana, agricultural assembly plant was walled off, and assembly of the prototypes began. The fifty-hour test runs required of these vehicles were conducted on the weekends, while the rest of the plant was idle.

Despite the 1A priority raring, the secretary's desired rapid development of the Ontos was not meeting his expectations. Only six pilot vehicles had been completed by midsummer 1952. The first of these, T55 number 1, was shipped to Aberdeen Proving Ground (in Maryland) on May 26, 1952. The second T55 was shipped to Fort Knox on June 18, and the first T166 was shipped to Aberdeen on July 1, which was also the destination of the first T165, which was shipped on July 18. The first T56 was shipped to Fort Knox on July 30, while the second was dispatched to Aberdeen on August 19.

Testing of the T56 at Fort Knox indicated that the vehicle was too cramped to be effective, while its competitor, the FMC T59, was more spacious and better armored, and work on the T56 was halted.

Ontos was actually the name of a series of five types of vehicle developed in the early 1950s and based on a common chassis, of which only the M50/M50A1 went into full production. The series included two models of prototype personnel carrier: the T55, shown here, capable of carrying six men, and the longer T56, which held ten men. *Patton Museum*

Supplement number 3 to the Ontos contract was issued on January 14, 1953. This change resulted in the breakdown of prototypes to be as follows:

(1) two vehicles, T55 (six-man personal carrier)
(2) two vehicles, T56 (ten-man personnel carrier)
(3) eleven vehicles, T165 (six rifles)
(4) three vehicles, T166 (one rifle)

A further change on January 19 authorized the number of six-rifle armed vehicles to be increased to twenty-four. However, these were to be a new variant, the T165E1, and it featured improved armament. The M27 105 mm recoilless rifle carried by previous Ontos test vehicles gave way to the T170 recoilless rifle (later standardized as the M40). While officially classified as a 106 mm weapon, in reality it too was 105 mm, with the stated difference in bore being an effort to prevent mixing of the incompatible M27 and M40 munitions. The M40 was designated at battalion antitank weapon, or BAT. Like development of the Ontos, the development and testing of the BAT had lagged behind schedule.

Some of the existing T165 pilots were brought up to T165E1 standards and subjected to tests, and the first of the T166 pilots was converted to a T165E1 as well. Those tests indicated further improvements were needed, particularly to the track and suspension, and accordingly a change order directed that the fifteen new-build machines, serial numbers 10 through 24, incorporate these improvements and be designated T165E2. The improved suspension system of the T165E2 featured dual rubber-tired steel road wheels rather than the previously used pneumatic tires.

The pilot 106 mm Self-propelled Rifle T166 consisted of a single 106 mm Rifle T170E1 on a pedestal roof on the roof of a Tracked Utility Vehicle T55. Mounted above the recoilless rifle barrel is a .50-caliber spotting rifle. The US Army registration number stenciled near the top of the superstructure is 40232487. *TACOM LCMC History Office*

Another member of the Ontos family was the T165 multiple, self-propelled 105 mm rifle. Despite that designation, it actually had six 106 mm T170E1 recoilless rifles. These were mounted on a cross-shaft extending from the small turret. A driver, gunner, and loader made up the three-man crew. *Ordnance Museum*

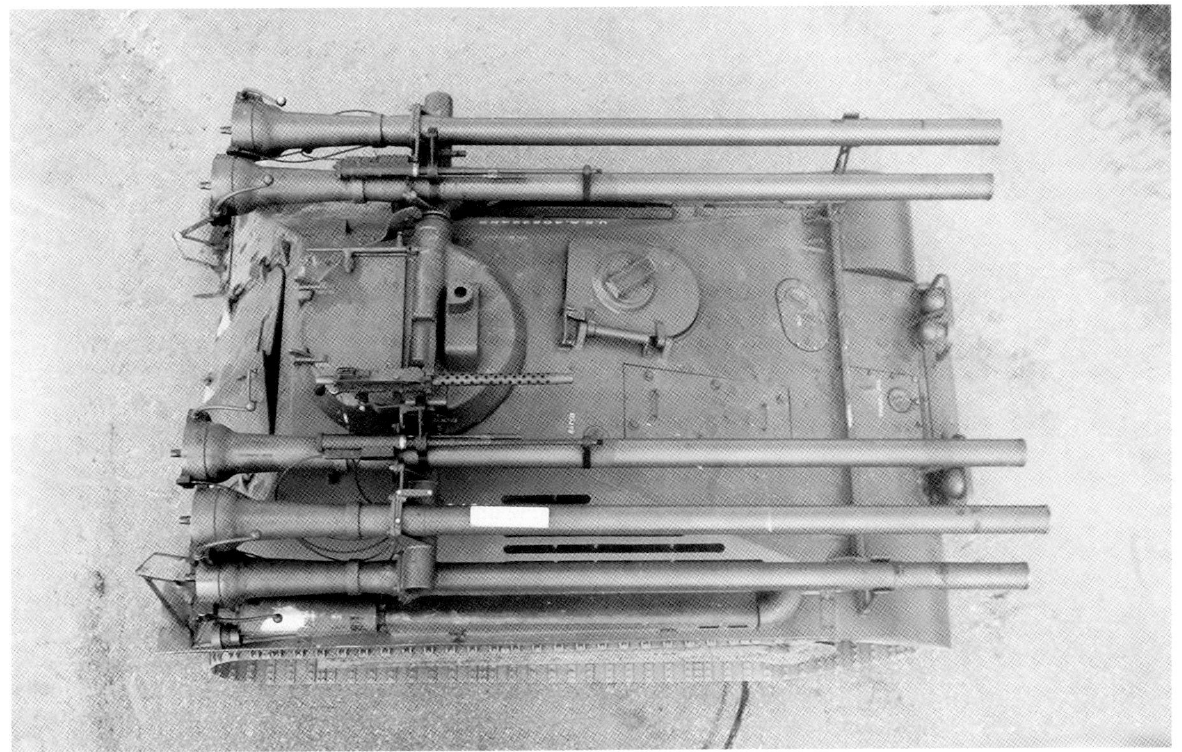

The driver of the T165 sat toward the front left of the hull, next to the General Motors model 302 six-cylinder in-line gasoline engine. The T170E1 106 mm recoilless rifles are resting on the folding travel lock, and a .30-caliber machine gun is to the side of the gunner's hatch on top of the turret. *Ordnance Museum*

The recoilless rifles are shown at maximum traverse and elevation. Mounted above the upper four weapons were .50-caliber spotting rifles that fired M48 spotter-tracer rounds with approximately the same trajectory as the 106 mm projectiles. The gunner could use the fire of the spotting rifles to make adjustments to the big guns before committing them. *Ordnance Museum*

A T165 (note the lack of ventilation louvers on the glacis) at Aberdeen Proving Ground on July 26, 1952, demonstrates the recoilless rifles at maximum depression and maximum right traverse. An M1919 .30-caliber machine gun is visible over the .50-caliber spotting rifle on the right side. The recoilless rifles were mounted on a transverse metal tube with open ends. *Ordnance Museum*

The front of the hull of the T165 lacked ventilation grilles for the engine, since the prominent louvers on the right side of the hull served that purpose. Two doors at the rear of the hull provided access to the gunner's compartment. Below the doors was a compartment for storing eight rounds of 106 mm ammunition. *Patton Museum*

A rear view of a T165 at Aberdeen Proving Ground on July 26, 1952, shows the low turret that supported the six 106 mm recoilless rifles. Above the rear mudguards are frames that served as stops for the two rear doors. Below the rear doors is the door for the ammunition storage compartment. *Ordnance Museum*

The rear doors of the fighting compartment are open on this T165 photographed at Aberdeen on July 26, 1952, exposing some of the interior to view, including the gunner's seat and controls and vertical supports for the roof. The vision port on the left door would be moved to the right door on production M50s. *Ordnance Museum*

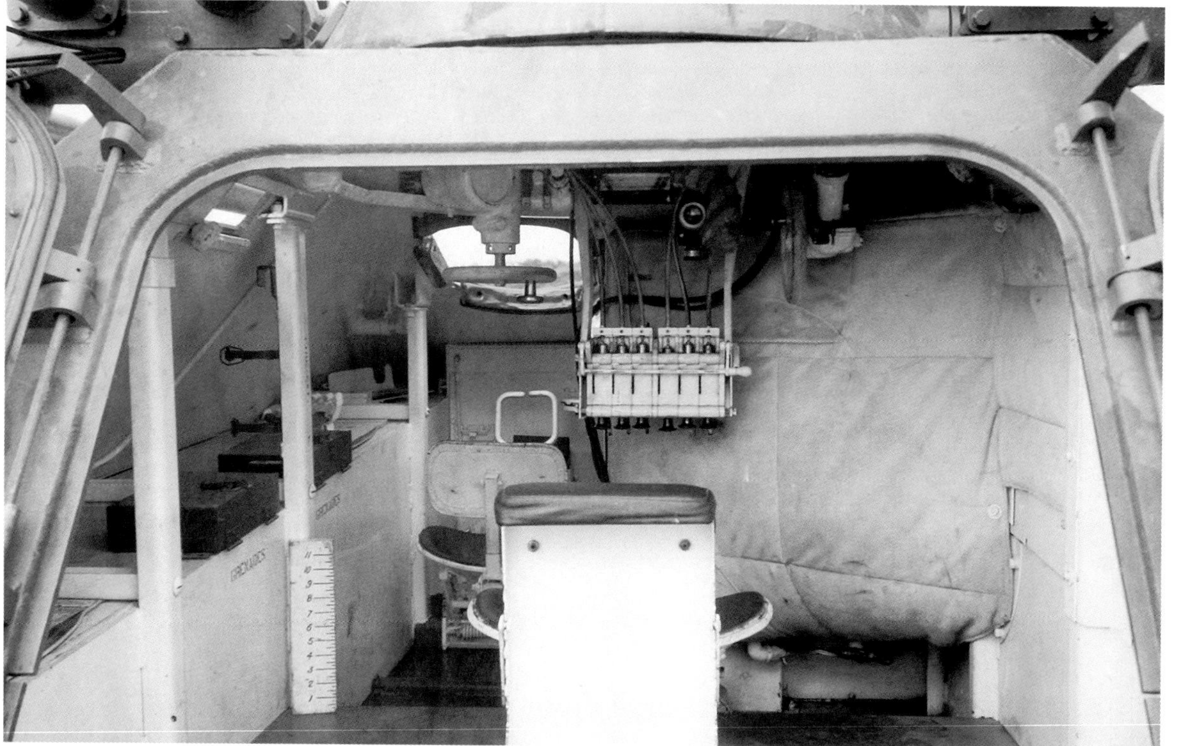

As viewed through the rear door, the interior of the T165 was cramped, with the gunner's seat toward the rear and the driver's seat in the narrow compartment to the left of the engine. The first T165 was completed on July 18, 1952, and the vehicle was one of the pilots of the M50 Ontos. *Ordnance Museum*

In the summer of 1954, the Detroit Arsenal experimented with a quadruple .50-caliber antiaircraft machine-gun mount on an Ontos chassis with a cut-down superstructure. The mount was provided with "batwing" armored shields *TACOM LCMC History Office*

On close inspection, the batwing shields on the quadruple .50-caliber machine gun mount were mockups made of thin wood with cabinet hinges. A raised panel with cooling louvers was installed on the right side of the glacis. *TACOM LCMC History Office*

Two T55 Ontos-based "Utility Vehicle, Full Tracked, Infantry, T55" were produced. The first of these, registration number 40232481, was shipped to Detroit Arsenal in March 1955, where an enlarged cargo/passenger compartment was installed, as seen in a photo taken in September 1955. To achieve the conversion, part of the superstructure was cut away, and a driver's hood and a boxy enclosure with windows were installed. The driver's hood had a heated windshield with an electrical wiper, and a small window on each side. Baggage racks and a spotlight were on the roof. The muffler and tailpipe were repositioned vertically near the right front of the new enclosure. The vehicle was subsequently used during Operation Deep Freeze 1. *TACOM LCMC History Office*

T165 registration number 40232482 is shown in a June 20, 1953, photograph taken for the Detroit Arsenal. The side channel alongside the bogie wheels helped support the suspension. To the front of the pioneer tool rack is the welded-on hood for a ventilation blower. Below the lower rear corner of the tool rack is the right taillight. *TACOM LCMC History Office*

During Armor Board testing at Fort Knox, an M50 is resting in deep mud alongside a pond. Canvas covers are secured over the recoilless rifles. The number "142" is stenciled in white on the left mudguard. *Kevin Emdee collection*

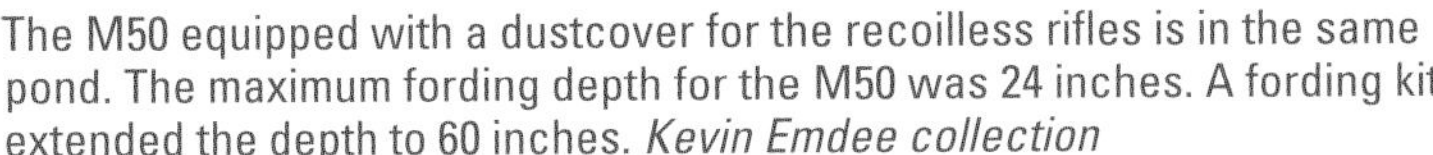

The M50 equipped with a dustcover for the recoilless rifles is in the same pond. The maximum fording depth for the M50 was 24 inches. A fording kit extended the depth to 60 inches. *Kevin Emdee collection*

A soldier wearing a fatigue cap is standing in the top hatch of an M50 Ontos as it attempts to negotiate a very muddy bank during a field test or exercise. These dustcovers are rarely seen in photographs of the Ontos. *Kevin Emdee collection*

A Detroit Arsenal photo dated May 23, 1957, depicts one of fifteen T165E2 pilots, which incorporated improvements mandated by earlier testing of the T165E1s. The T165E2s featured dual open-spoked wheels with solid rubber tires. The ventilation louvers for the engine compartment had been moved from the right side of the superstructure to the right side of the glacis. At this point in the vehicle's development, the muffler on the right side of the superstructure lacked a shield. Exposed wiring harnesses for firing the rifles are in view. *TACOM LCMC History Office*

The "T165E1 Rifle, Multiple, 106 mm, Self-Propelled" was an improved version of the pilot T165. Production of this version was authorized in February 1953, and twenty-four examples were ordered, with the last fifteen of them later being built to different specifications and redesignated the T165E2. The T165E1 mounted six T170A1 106 mm recoilless rifles and two T46E1 .50-caliber spotting rifles on elevating arms extending from the sides of the small turret. These mounts for the 106 mm rifles were similar to those employed on the preceding T165 pilot vehicle but were significantly different in appearance from the mounts that would be installed on the production M50 Ontos. The front-to-back-oriented, slotted louvers on the glacis were a characteristic of the T165E1.

On the front right side (as viewed by the driver when facing forward) of the T165E1 are the small blackout marker light and the right service headlight, protected by a brush guard. Missing from its mount next to that headlight is the horn. On the driver's left are the blackout driving headlight, left service headlight, and blackout marker light. The engine access door is the plain panel with a handle and two hinges below and to the side of the driver's hatch; it was locked in place with latch bolts. The driver's hatch door, or cover in official parlance, is hinged to the upper center of the glacis and has a counterbalancing torsion spring to assist in opening and closing. A periscope with brush guard is also part of the driver's hatch cover. On the front of the lower hull are two towing lugs with shackles attached.

The profile of the slide-in/bolt-on cast 105 mm rifle mount, unique to the T165E1, is apparent in this photo. The beam running along the outsides of the road wheels is the side channel, which gave extra rigidity and strength to the suspension and provided a mounting for the shock absorbers.

The circular object toward the bottom center of the photo is the transmission oil filler cover. At the center of the photo above the cross-shaft of the travel lock is the fuel pump cover, which also incorporates the fuel tank filler access cover.

External elements of the exhaust are mounted on the right side only, with an expanded-steel mesh shield covering much of it. At the upper left are the taillight and guard and the breech lever of the lower-right recoilless rifle.

On the right side of the upper hull of the T165E1 above the exhaust, muffler, and muffler guard are, left to right, the right taillight and guard, pioneer tool rack with mattock head, a bulge to provide clearance for the oil-bath air cleaner, and the air cleaner service door. The construction of the fender and its supports is visible.

The Ontos has had two types of drive sprocket. During development, a multisection rubberized solid sprocket was tested. This T165E1 is the only known surviving example of this initial rubber-coated developmental sprocket. A more conventional multisection sprocket comprising an inner and outer sprocket mounting on a hub would replace this initial sprocket with the upgrade to the T165E2 and the production M50/M50A1.

The rear of the hull of the T165E1 was similar in design to that of the M50, except for the arrangement of the vision port and the outside locking handle. The T165E1 has the vision port on the left, primarily due to developmental plans for the stowing of a recoilless-rifle tripod on the inside of the left door. This arrangement left too little room for the loader, so on the M50/M50A1 the tripod was removed and the vision port and outside locking-handle position were reversed.

The Ontos' recoilless rifles were assigned numbers, left to right (facing them from the rear), with number "1" to the lower left and number "6" to the lower right. The frameworks to the sides of both doors are doorstops; the latches just above the bend lines on the doors engage the stops when open, preventing the doors from inadvertently slamming shut.

This T165E1 features the early track-adjusting idler (rear road wheel). The process of maintaining track tension was improved with the T165E2 and the addition of a tensioner bracket that extended from the side channel. The more durable track tension assembly is seen on production Ontos as a side channel extension with adjusting screws.

The gunner's periscope has been removed from the front of the turret of this T165E1, and the opening has been covered. To the left is the cradle and ammunition box holder for a .30-caliber machine gun, which was affixed to the recoilless-rifle mount to fire coaxially.

Viewing the gunner's hatch cover from the rear, to the left is the door's hold-open rod. The button-shaped object on top of the rod is a plunger, which acted to lock the holder in place. To the upper right is the cradle and ammunition box holder for the coaxial .30-caliber machine gun.

As seen from the left side, the sliding design of the hold-open rod on the gunner's hatch cover is visible, with its outer sleeve, plunger, and inner rod. A mounting lug for the rod is cast into the housing of the cross-shaft of the recoilless-rifle mounts. To the lower right, at the center top of the rear of the hull, is the radio antenna mount.

As seen from the left side, the gunner's hatch cover is a smooth steel plate. To open the door, the two interior handles were turned and the door was lifted until the plunger on the hold-open rod engaged the stop in the rod. Pulling the plunger unlocked it so the door could be closed.

Further details of the construction and appearance of the top of the turret are presented. Weld lines, the rough-cast surface of the turret, and the cross-shaft housing are visible. At the lower left is the upper corner of the driver's hatch cover, showing its top hinge and the door's hold-open latch.

The right side of the recoilless-rifle mount lacked the detents and limiting flange that were present on the left side of the mount. Built into the rear of both of the door hinges are horn-shaped doorstops that acted in concert with the hold-open rod to limit the rearward travel of the door when open.

CHAPTER 2

The Ontos Enters Production

Following the production of several T165 prototypes, twenty-four improved T165E1 and T165E2 prototypes were built before the vehicle was standardized as the M50 Ontos. At a secret Allis-Chalmers assembly line in La Porte, Indiana, a number of Ontos are under construction. In the background is a hull bearing the USMC registration number 226706. *Patton Museum*

On January 9, 1953, less than two weeks before Frank Pace's term as secretary of the Army was to end, he was briefed on the status of the BAT and Ontos. Testing during the preceding four months had shown both items to be deficient. The problems with the BAT were relatively minor, and the Army chief of staff, Gen. Lawton Collins, recommended that production of the recoilless rifle begin. The Ontos' problems were more complex, and Gen. Collins's recommendation was that production not begin until after service tests had been completed, and even then, rather than the thousands advocated by Project Vista, only three hundred be purchased for field testing in Europe and Korea.

The US Marine Corps had been provided one of the T165E2 pilots for testing. On April 9, 1954, Gen. Lemuel C. Shepherd Jr., commandant of the Marine Corps, stated that the pilot, with some modification, had reached minimum combat acceptability.

The desired modifications included changing the fire control system such that individual components could be replaced in the field, further reinforcing the suspension, including provisions for the installation of a deepwater-fording kit and use of the Allison XT-90-2 transmission.

The pilot was so modified, and on November 23, Gen. Shepherd considered the vehicle, with minor changes to the pilot, to be an acceptable prototype for production. Following a coordination meeting on December 1, Shepherd indicated that the Marine Corps was ready to place an initial order for 250 of the vehicles.

The Army, on the other hand, was not as pleased with the vehicle. On March 1, 1955, the chief of Ordnance was sent the final report of testing on the T165E2, which in its summary said the vehicle was "unsuitable for use by field forces." Elaborating, the report stated that the vehicle lacked mechanical reliability and had inadequate space for crew and ammunition, poor accuracy, and limited protection. Of concern was that to reload the six weapons, a crewman had to exit the vehicle.

It is somewhat ironic that the Army deemed the Ontos as unsuitable in part due to the limited protection it provided the crew, yet they approved the totally open M56 Scorpion antitank gun, upon which the crew was exposed not only during reloading, but all the time.

Despite Army use being out of the picture, on March 24, 1955, Ordnance classified the Ontos as "Standard" for the Marine Corps, designating the vehicle "Rifle, Multiple, 106mm, Self-Propelled, M50." That same day, Army development on the project was terminated.

On August 12, 1955, fixed-price contract 11-022-1849, valued at $13,249,727, was awarded to Allis-Chalmers Manufacturing Company to produce the Ontos. The vehicles would be built in La Porte, Indiana, in a 2.5-million-dollar facility that had been

A mechanic standing in the hatch of an Ontos makes an adjustment in the engine compartment while another mechanic works on the drive sprocket. The thinness of the frontal armor is evident. It was ½-inch rolled homogeneous steel, suitable only for repelling shrapnel and small-arms fire. *La Porte County Historical Society*

built earlier, in 1951, for the production of the M8 high-speed tractor. That Allis-Chalmers-operated facility was immediately adjacent to the company's harvester plant.

At the time the contract was announced, it was stated that production was to begin in August 1956 and last one year, but the number of vehicles to be built was secret. That veil of secrecy was short-lived, since an October 1956 publication by Lukens Steel, a firm that supplied "32 items of armor plate made to military specifications for the Ontos. Plate items include side and front plates, both fenders and the hatch cover," stated that "Allis-Chalmers in LaPorte, Ind., is building 293 of these machines."

Also changing was the production schedule, as evidenced by a story in the November 1, 1956, *South Bend Tribune*, which reported, "Maj. Gen. Edward W. Snedeker, assistant chief of staff, US Marine Corps, accepts delivery of the first production model of the Ontos, a compact and highly maneuverable anti-tank weapon, from Robert S. Stevenson, president of Allis-Chalmers Manufacturing Co., at the LaPorte Works of Allis-Chalmers Wednesday."

An article in the November 30, 1956, *Indianapolis News* stated that "Allis-Chalmers will begin turning out thirty units a month within a couple of weeks under a $13 million defense contract."

The speed with which production began was subject to some scrutiny and criticism concerning questionable use of a price redetermination clause in the contract. In testimony before Congress, the Army, which had issued the contract on behalf of the Marine Corps, stated, "Ordnance Corps was aware of the situation in this case which developed due to an urgent requirement expressed by United States Marine Corps for production of rifle, multiple 106 millimeter, self-propelled, M50 [ONTOS]. Actions taken because of this situation were not standard procurement procedures and explanations of the actions taken were provided DCSLOG [deputy chief of staff for logistics] in writing on November 1 and 2, 1956:

Late in 1955, faced with a mid-1956 target for production of ONTOS and a situation where a portion of necessary engineering was out of phase with the other actions required, Ordnance took steps to employ incomplete Research and Development drawings available under a Frankford Arsenal design contract (ORD-359 with Harvey Machine Co.).

The first step in this approach was to have the contractor providing the design drawings revise his format to supply production type drawings to the best of his ability on the engineering data then available. The type of design contract and the manner of funding did not permit his completion of this approach but did enable production of a significant portion of the drawings required in a comparatively short period of time.

Recognizing that the design contractor could not complete the job, arrangements were made with the vehicle engineering agency (Allis-Chalmers Co.) to assume complete responsibility

A worker at Allis-Chalmers' La Porte, Indiana, plant is assembling a component in the fighting compartment of an M50 Ontos. To his front is the radiator. The driver's seat and hatch are in the left front of the vehicle. Inside the rear door, below the worker's forearms, is a clamp, which forms the rear rack for four rounds of ammunition for the 106 mm recoilless rifles. On the upper part of the right door is a vision port, with a sliding door with locking knobs. A knob for operating the hold-open latch is present on the lower part of each door. *USMC*

The mechanic has installed the transmission cover and front air intake louver immediately to the rear of the right headlight assembly. For ventilating the engine compartment, the production M50s dispensed with the large louvers on the right side of the hull in favor of louvered panels on the glacis. *La Porte County Historical Society*

for the weapons-control system drawings. To accomplish this work in the limited time available, it was necessary for the VEA to work overtime and to subcontract for further drawing completion with the original design contractor.

Since actions taken by Ordnance in this case were founded upon the urgency of delivery of ONTOS to United States Marine Corps, use of the preliminary release approach for engineering was necessary to enable provision of adequate procurement leadtime for the item. Utilization of this approach was followed to permit Ordnance to meet the July 1956 start of production target. To have handled the problem otherwise would have resulted in delaying the start of production date to April or May 1957.

It has been estimated that the cost of obsolescence will not exceed $50,000. Had engineering been covered by final releases, experience has indicated that the degree of obsolescence would have been approximately the same, and, in addition, the entire program would have been delayed by 10 months. Therefore, it is believed that Ordnance used the most reasonable and expedient method possible in handling the program in the manner described.

The M50 was powered by the 145-horsepower GMC 302-cubic-inch, six-cylinder engine, which drove through an Allison XT-90-2 transmission, giving it a top speed of 30 miles per hour.

The main armament of the Ontos was six M40A1C 106 mm recoilless rifles mounted externally on an extremely low-profile turret, which afforded 40 degrees of traverse to either side of center, and an elevation range of −10 through +20 degrees. In addition to the rounds carried in the chambers of each rifle, there was stowage for four rounds in the right rear of the crew compartment and a further eight rounds in a compartment in the lower hull.

In addition to the six recoilless rifles, the upper outboard of which were both demountable for use on provided ground tripods, the Ontos was armed with an M1919A4 .30-caliber machine gun. The machine gun could be locked into place and fired from inside the Ontos as a coaxial weapon, or it could be fired manually and flexibly by a gunner standing in the hatch. Rifles 2, 3, 4, and 5 each were equipped with M8C .50-caliber spotting rifles, the bullets of which had a trajectory similar to that of the M40C recoilless rifle through the effective range of the recoilless. The rifles could be fired individually, in pairs, or all at once. Recoilless

Three women pose in front of a newly minted M50 at the Allis-Chalmers plant. The six recoilless rifles are at about maximum elevation, and the air intake louvers are removed, exposing the engine compartment to view. Also noticeable is the expanded steel mesh guard over the muffler. While the original caption of this photo has been lost, some observations can be made. The carefully posed photo is characteristic of a special occasion. Chalked on the hull, to the rear of the exhaust pipe is a partially legible number. By enlarging the image it can be seen that the three-digit number begins with 29—and the final digit is either 3 or 5. Since there were 293 documented M50s built, it is likely this image captures the final example leaving the assembly line. *La Porte County Historical Society*

A right-front view of an M50 106 mm self-propelled multiple rifle at the Detroit Arsenal on October 30, 1959, discloses fine details of the headlights and brush guards, the travel lock and its operating link, the engine-access doors / cooling louvers, the exhaust pipe and muffler, and the recoilless-rifle mounts. *TACOM LCMC History Office*

A GI wearing a tank crewman's helmet of World War II vintage is posing next to an Ontos. The barrels of the two bottom 106 mm recoilless rifles are clamped in travel locks. Each of the two headlight arrays includes a service headlight at the center and a blackout marker lamp on the outboard side. A horn is on the inboard side of the right array, and a blackout headlight is on the inboard side of the left array.

First Sgt. Culp, US Army, poses next to an M50 at the Detroit Arsenal on January 30, 1960. The registration number near the rear of the superstructure, 226672, painted yellow, is a USMC number. Spare track crossbar and guide assemblies and what appears to be a muffler shield are on the side of the superstructure, flanking the liquid-container holder.

Lying on the pavement in front of an Ontos ready for inspection is an array of vehicular equipment. Among the gear in the foreground are headphone sets; two M27 tripods with M92 rifle mounts on top, for firing two of the recoilless rifles dismounted from the vehicle; an M3A1 Grease Gun submachine gun; and mechanics' tools, including sockets, Allen wrenches, open-ended wrenches, ball peen hammer, and screwdrivers. In the background are a rolled camouflage net, flashlights, first-aid kit, 5-gallon liquid container, binoculars, disassembled rammer staff, and rammer heads. The two upper outboard 106 mm rifles, designated numbers 2 and 5, along with their .50-caliber spotting rifles, could be detached from their cradles and emplaced on the M27 tripods and M92 mounts for firing on the ground. The M27 tripods and M92 rifle mounts were not transported in the Ontos but in a support vehicle. *La Porte County Historical Society*

rifles generate a considerable amount of backblast, and in the case of the Ontos, firing all six rifles at once, the unsafe area behind the vehicle was a cone measuring 100 feet deep and 350 feet wide at its base. The Ontos was equipped with AN/VRC-8 and AN/PRC-10 radios but, due to its small size, no intercom. The vehicle was served by a three-man crew of driver, loader, and gunner, all of whom were considered by the USMC to be infantrymen rather than armor crewmen.

Production of the M50 was completed on November 30, 1957.

The Marines assigned the Ontos to regimental antitank companies, each consisting of a dozen Ontos, five officers, and ninety-one enlisted men. Each company was divided into three platoons, with four vehicles apiece. This was later increased to five vehicles, for a total of fifteen Ontos per regimental antitank company.

The first operational use of the Ontos outside of training exercises came on July 15–16, 1958, when Battalion Landing Teams 2/2 and 3/6 landed in Beirut, Lebanon. The 2nd Provisional Marine Force, under Brig. Gen. Sidney Wade, first took control of the airport, then the port and bridges over the Beirut River, and enhanced security at the US embassy. The Lebanese army was cooperative, and Wade's fifteen M48s, ten Ontos, and thirty-one LVTP-5 amtracs did not see combat. The Marines began to withdraw on August 14 after having been relieved by an Army medium-tank battalion.

USMC colonel D. J. Robinson, Ordnance Branch, G-4, HQMC, and Brig. Gen. H. C. Tschirgi, assistant chief of staff, G-4, USMC, engaged in the following dialogue with Congressman Robert Sikes before the House Subcommittee on Appropriations in 1961:

Mr. Sikes: Tell me something about the ONTOS program. Why did you buy it when the Army did not? The Army has terminated development.

Gen. Tschirgi: This vehicle was developed along in 1953 and 1954. It was developed concurrently or jointly by the Marine Corps and the Army. As you may recall, the vehicle has six rifles on it, 106 millimeter, recoilless. The vehicle weighs about 8 tons.

Mr. Sikes: Let me give you a few items. Vehicle is considered primarily defensive, has limited offensive capability. Effective range too short. Inadequate staying power on the battlefield. Vehicle could fire only six rounds before the crew must dismount

Following the testing of the T165E1 and T165E2 prototypes, the vehicle was standardized as the "Rifle, Self-Propelled, Full, Tracked, Multiple 106 mm, M50"—commonly known as the Ontos. Allis-Chalmers was issued a $13.25 million contract on August 12, 1955, to produce 297 of the vehicles for the US Marine Corps. The final vehicle of this contract was delivered on November 30, 1957. Modifications to this model that had been made since the pilot T165 included a redesigned exhaust, dual road wheels with solid rubber tires instead of single wheels with inflatable rubber tires, redesigned tracks, and the elimination of the louvers on the right side of the upper hull in favor of removable louvered air-intake panels on the glacis. *USMC*

to reload. Requirement for concealment, no provision for blast, short effective range made it impractical for infantry. If it is as bad as that, why do you want it?

Col. Robinson: In 1951, the Marine Corps had an urgent requirement for a midrange antimechanized weapon to be used at regimental and battalion level. At that time there was no effective weapon available other than the ONTOS, which was being developed at that time, and a 90-millimeter M-56. We tested out pilot models of the ONTOS and the Army did likewise. All the deficiencies that were developed during the tests were corrected prior to the production run. We bought the ONTOS primarily because there was nothing else available at that time to do the job.

Mr. Sikes: Are you buying any now?

Col. Robinson: We made a one-time procurement for Marine Corps requirements.

Mr. Sikes: You are not buying them now?

Col. Robinson: That is true. We are not.

Mr. Sikes. It was the weapon you needed at the time it was available and when there was nothing else?

Col. Robinson: That is correct.

The "Rifle, Self-Propelled, Full, Tracked, Multiple 106 mm, M50," as standardized, was armed with six recoilless rifles (model M40A1C) and spotting rifles as M8C. Another feature of the M50 was the bulge to the front of the pioneer tool rack; this provided clearance for the oil-bath air cleaner inside the engine compartment. Powering the M50 was the GMC 302 gasoline engine, linked to the Allison XT-90-2 transmission. *USMC*

With the travel lock folded down and the recoilless rifles at the ready, the Ontos presents a formidable appearance for a vehicle of its small size. The 106 mm recoilless rifles had a traverse of 40 degrees to either side of the centerline. Thus, it was necessary to execute major shifts in the aiming of the guns by moving the entire vehicle. These rifles had a maximum elevation of 20 degrees and could be depressed to −10 degrees. One of the primary vulnerabilities of the Ontos was that after the six rifles had fired, it was necessary for the loader to leave what little armored protection the vehicle offered, and reload the rifles outside. Thus, the usual practice was to move to a safer position, if feasible, to reload and resume fire. The firing of the rifles, however, was accomplished by the commander/gunner inside the Ontos. *USMC*

In 1957, several Marines inspect a newly delivered Ontos, evidently a T165E2. Although the 106 mm recoilless rifles on the left side of the Ontos appear at first glance to be tilted outward, this illusion is due to the angle of the turret, since the cradles of the rifles were not traversable on their mounts. *Naval History and Heritage Command*

This official photo of an Ontos highlights the layout of the glacis and the design of the tracks. The air-intake panels have the front-to-rear-oriented louvers characteristic of the T165E2. The tubular support for the .30-caliber machine gun over the turret, a feature of the M50, is not present. *Naval History and Heritage Command*

On the M50, a new mount for the M1919A4. 30-caliber machine gun was devised, centered over the front of the gunner's hatch on a U-shaped tubular bracket. On this Ontos, the machine gun is not installed, but the spotting rifles are in place over the recoilless rifles. *La Porte County Historical Society*

The blasts of the 106 mm recoilless rifles illuminate a Marine Corps M50 Ontos during a nighttime exercise in October 1955. The spotting rifle is not mounted on the clamps above the right outboard recoilless rifle.

Marines at Quantico, Virginia, are field-testing an Ontos in early December 1955. This was likely a pilot of the T165 family, since the contract for series production of the M50s was not issued until mid-August 1955, and the first Marine Corps acceptance of an M50 would not be until October 1956.

LCpl. B. D. Cash of C Company, 1st Antitank Battalion, 1st Marine Division, explains the workings of the Ontos to two young women at an exposition in Southern California. To the rear of the muzzles on the undersides of the two lowest 106 mm rifle barrels are the rifle shoes that helped secure the barrels in the travel lock. *USMC*

During the Heliflex IV-57 exercises at Camp Pendleton on March 28, 1957, the driver of an M50 Ontos, Pfc. John G. Corey, and gunner Pfc. Wallace R. Cooper of B "Ontos" Company, 1st Antitank Battalion, 1st Marine Division, are at their stations. The track sag is considerably more than the prescribed 1½ to 2½ inches. *USMC*

An Ontos precedes an M67 Patton flamethrower tank during maneuvers at Camp Lejeune, North Carolina, in May 1957. At this point, the Ontos had been in service for less than a year, and the Corps was just beginning to develop tactics for it. This vehicle has the tubular support for the .30-caliber machine gun but lacks the ventilation louvers on the glacis. *USMC*

A USMC M50 is silhouetted against an atomic cloud ten minutes after the test explosion of a nuclear bomb at the Nevada Proving Ground, outside Desert Rock, Nevada, on July 5, 1957. The vehicle was assigned to the 4th Marine Corps Atomic Exercises Brigade.

Two of the three crew members of a 1st Marine Division Ontos are in view during maneuvers at Camp Pendleton, California, around April 1958. On the inside of the driver's hatch door are a grab handle, a rotating periscope, and the lock handle. To the front of the driver's face are linkages for operating the travel lock for the recoilless rifles.

Around early April 1958, two Marine Ontos crews pose in front of their vehicles, with their equipment arranged neatly for inspection. In addition to such essentials as ramming staffs and rammers, tools, 5-gallon liquid containers, pioneer tools, duffel bags, and ammunition boxes, packing cases for the requisite eighteen rounds of 106 mm ammunition per vehicle are present. To the front of the crewmen are the M27 tripods with M92 rifle mounts for dismounted firing of the recoilless rifles, as well as the M1919A4 .30-caliber machine guns on tripod mounts. The white, double-tong-shaped implement in the foreground is a track-removal tool, officially designated Fixture 878108. All the crewmen are wearing CVC helmets, which provided ear protection as well as headphones and microphones for communicating via intercom: a necessity in a noisy operating environment. *USMC*

In mid-July 1958, a US amphibious force landed at Beirut, Lebanon. It was a military effort to intervene in a civil war between Christian and Muslim forces and was the United States' first combat experience in the Middle East. As part of that invasion, an Ontos is crossing Red Beach at Beirut on July 16, 1958. In addition to the three crewmen wearing tank-crew helmets, a fourth Marine wearing a fatigue cap is sitting on a camouflage net on the front of the vehicle.

In an undated photograph, a T165E2 Ontos crew conducts a training exercise at Quantico, Virginia. The loader is inserting a 106 mm round into one of the rifles while the gunner looks on. Operating the breech mechanism required a coordinated effort between the gunner, manning controls within the vehicle, and the loader, working outside the vehicle. *USMC*

A loader pushes a 106 mm round into the breech. All the manual operating handles of the breeches are turned to the rear, indicating that all three breeches in view are open. The recoilless rifles on the Ontos fired various types of ammunition, including the high-explosive plastic–tracer (HEP-T), high-explosive antitank (HEAT), and "beehive" antipersonnel ordnance. *USMC*

An Ontos platoon lands on a beach and prepares to move inland. Each Ontos platoon comprised three M50s in a heavy section and two M50s in a light section. Three platoons made up a company, and three companies constituted a battalion. *USMC*

An M50 from the 3rd Marine Division has disembarked from a landing craft along the northern coast of Borneo in June 1959. This evidently was part of Operation Saddle Up, a joint US-British training exercise that included the 1st Battalion, 1st Marine Regiment, 3rd Marine Division. Wooden locks have been fitted over the recoilless-rifle barrels, to protect them from jarring, and covers have been installed over the rears of those weapons. Another Ontos is on the deck of the landing craft. Both vehicles are marked "C2" on the right mudguards.

A line of Ontos are parked at the 1st Marine Division's antitank battalion vehicle park at Camp Pendleton, California, in April 1958. The original caption of this official photograph boasted that the 106 mm recoilless rifles could penetrate any enemy tank, but by the early 1960s that claim would no longer be true. *Naval History and Heritage Command*

An Ontos treks through deep snow in California's Sierra Nevada during cold-weather training exercises in March 1958. The vehicle was assigned to the 1st Marine Division, Fleet Marine Force, at Camp Pendleton, California. The vehicle number B33 is painted on the right rear door. *USMC*

The same Ontos, number B33, appears in a different position. Ontos operators were instructed to avoid driving up and down grades and making sharp turns on crusty snow and were told to drive in low gear on powdery snow. The Ontos would see combat in climes very different from this semi-Alpine scene. *USMC*

During training exercises at the Marine Corps Schools at Quantico, Virginia, on March 20, 1961, an M67 flamethrower tank streams fire while a supporting infantry squad and an M50 Ontos stand by, waiting. Infantrymen had to take care not to be to the rear of the Ontos if it was likely to be firing its recoilless rifles, since the backblast was devastating. *USMC*

From the onset, the Ontos was conceived as air transportable and was designed to fit in the cargo holds of US transport aircraft. In 1961 at the Marine Corps Air Facility (MCAF) New River, North Carolina, a driver backs an Ontos up the ramp of a GV-1 (later, C-130B) Hercules, following hand signals of a crewman. It was an extremely tight fit. *USMC*

Two members of the US Marine Corps Reserve were photographed on an Ontos during training exercises at Camp Lejeune. Protruding from the recoilless rifle at the top left is the cover for the optical sight, the M92D elbow telescope, which was used when the dismountable recoilless rifles were used in ground-mounted situations. *USMC*

Personnel of the 2nd Antitank Team and the 2nd Shore Party, elements of the 2nd Marine Division, Fleet Marine Force (FMF), at Camp Lejeune, worked together to devise this sling for hoisting the Ontos. Several spreader bars kept the steel cables properly positioned. Each of the cable eyes was fastened to two shackles, which in turn were secured to the lifting lugs on the hull. It was sometimes necessary to hoist the Ontos for placing it on transport vehicles or ships, and the previous method of hoisting it had frequently resulted in damage to the vehicle and the recoilless rifles. This sling reduced the chances for such damage. *USMC*

CHAPTER 3

The M50A1

Beginning with the fiscal year 1963 appropriations, the M50 was updated. The budget request presented to the House simply said, "the initiation of a modernization program for M103 heavy gun tank and the ONTOS, our antitank weapon." The fiscal year 1964 hearings before the House committee provide a little more detail, detailing that $3 million had been allocated in 1963 to issue a contract to Allis-Chalmers for "Rebuild and conversion, 106 mm self-propelled vehicle, rifle, M50 (ONTOS) to M50A1 configuration."

However, this contract was but the first, as reported in the February 8, 1963, edition of the *Journal and Courier* (Lafayette, Indiana): "The award was the first of a $9 million total earmarked for rebuilding self-propelled, track-lug vehicles mounting 106-millimeter guns. It was presumed, but not certain, the balance of the work also will be done at the LaPorte plant."

On June 29, 1963, the *South Bend Tribune* reported:

> A $3.4 million national defense contract to build and convert 294 Ontos armored military vehicle for the US Army Militarial Command was awarded Friday to Allis-Chalmers Mfg. Co. in LaPorte.
>
> The new contract, which brings to $6,830,000 the amount of defense contracts awarded to the plant this year, was announced by Congressman John Brademas.
>
> Brademas said the work will include interior modernization of the 106 millimeter self-propelled vehicle on which Allis-Chalmers has been working since 1955.
>
> Company officials said that the contract, made with the Chicago Procurement Division, includes a clause which would permit an additional $1,364,000 for the project scheduled for completion by the end of 1964.
>
> Modernization includes a more powerful engine for the vehicle for which replacement parts will be supplied.

The *Cincinnati Enquirer*, reporting on the same contract the same day, said, "Allis-Chalmers also received a US Army contract that provides an additional $3,415,000 for rebuilding and modernizing the 'Ontos' anti-tank vehicles at the LaPorte, Ind., plant. Total worth of the contract is $6,830,000. First half of the funds were received earlier this year."

The *Des Moines Register* provided an additional detail, with the report stating, "A second Army contract to Allis-Chalmers for $3,415,000 calls for modernization of 297 Ontos anti-tank vehicles that were built in 1955–57."

The "more powerful engine" referred to in the *South Bend Tribune* item was a Chrysler 361-cubic-inch V-8. The HT-361-318 developed 180 gross horsepower at 3,450 rpm and was coupled to a new Allison XT-90-5 transmission. To keep the new engine cool required redesigned armored engine covers. The new cover extended forward of the rifle's travel lock, and the engine access door gained louvers.

At the same time, the gunner's M20A3C periscope was replaced with an M20A3G periscope, and an M13A1C elevation quadrant was added. At the rear of the vehicle, a view port was added to the rear door.

On April 26, 1965, Battalion Landing Team (BLT) 3/6, the Caribbean Ready Force of the US Second Fleet, landed in Santo Domingo, Dominican Republic, where civil war was breaking out. Two days later a platoon each of tanks, amtracs, and two platoons of Ontos came ashore to reinforce the BLT. Although the Marines were taken under fire by snipers, rules of engagement prevented the Marines from responding with anything more than

The M50A1 Ontos was an improved model of the M50. The principal change was the upgrading of the power plant to the Chrysler HT-361-318 V-8 gasoline engine with the Allison XT-90-5 transmission. The new engine produced 180 gross horsepower at 3,540 rpm, netting the M50A1 a gain of 35 horsepower over the M50 at the expense of an added 80 pounds of overall vehicular weight. A key external change of the M50A1 was the introduction of ventilating louvers on the engine access door, below and to the right of the driver's hatch, and on the transmission cover, below the cross-shaft of the travel lock. Other minor changes included the adoption of the M92F elbow telescope for the ground-mount kit of the recoilless rifles and the replacement of the M20A3C gunner's periscope of the M50s with the M20A3G periscope. This M50A1 was photographed during acceptance testing at Aberdeen Proving Ground in March 1963. *La Porte County Historical Society*

infantry weapons. Fortunately, both sides agreed to a ceasefire that same day. More Marines and Ontos, as well as additional tanks and amtracs, arrived on May 7, but the ceasefire held. On June 5, the Marines withdrew.

But the landing in Santo Domingo was not the first for Marine Ontos in 1965. On March 8, the 9th Marine Expeditionary Brigade began landing in Đà Nẵng, Republic of Vietnam, bringing with them amtracs, tanks, and Ontos. In March 1966, the antitank battalion of the 1st Marine Division arrived, and in July 1966 the antitank battalion of the 3rd Marine Division was also in country. In the summer of 1967 these forces were augmented by a company from the 5th Antitank Battalion, which arrived with the 27th Marines.

Once in country, the Ontos units were initially deployed to defend the Đà Nẵng air base. However, on August 17, 1965, some Ontos took part in Operation Starlite, an amphibious assault south of Chu Lai intended as a preemptive strike against the Vietcong (VC) 1st Regiment, which was threatening the Chu Lai Air Base. During the course of the operation, a Marine armored column on Hill 30 was ambushed, with the lead M48 being damaged. An Ontos in the column maneuvered to provide frontal fire and to protect the flanks while artillery fire and air support were called in and the casualties were evacuated.

The Vietcong had for years extorted a "tax" on the farmers in the area of Marble Mountain near Đà Nẵng, seizing a percentage of their rice harvest. The September 1965 harvest would be different, with the Marines protecting the farmers working in their paddies, an effort dubbed Operation Golden Fleece. On September 12, Huynh Ba Trinh, chief of Hoa Hai village, informed Lt. Col. Verle E. Ludwig, commander of 1st Battalion, 9th Marines, that a VC main force unit had entered a hamlet south of Marble Mountain to collect its "rice tax." Ludwig responded by sending a two-company attack force, along with Ontos, tanks, and amtracs. The VC fired mortars and recoilless rifles but withdrew from the area, and during the remainder of the harvest it was punctuated by only occasional attempts by VC "tax collectors."

By December 1965, the III Marine Amphibious Force had in Vietnam sixty-five Ontos from the 1st and 3d Anti-Tank Battalions, as well as 157 LVTP-5 amphibious tractors (amtracs), sixty-five M48 90 mm gun tanks, and twelve M67 flame tanks.

Early in 1966, the Marines launched an effort to thwart VC operations on the Lòng Tàu River, near Saigon. Known as Operation Jack Stay, the operation began with a March 26 amphibious landing on Long Thanh Peninsula. To provide gunfire support for those landings, the Marines had three M50A1 Ontos aboard USS *Henry County* (LST-824) to serve as improvised naval gunfire.

At 0830 on the morning of June 29, 1966, a convoy of twenty-eight South Vietnamese marine trucks moving north on Route 1 was ambushed by the 802nd VC Battalion with automatic weapons, recoilless rifles, and mortars, hitting ten of the trucks. The Vietnamese marines dismounted and began returning fire against the superior VC force. The VC succeeded in dividing the South Vietnamese marine force into two groups, which were not mutually supporting. Fortunately, a US Army spotter plane flew overhead, and US Marine advisors accompanying the South Vietnamese marines were able to make radio contact with the Army aircraft, relaying their plight. Also monitoring the radio was 12th Marines, who launched an artillery strike, the first rounds landing at 0846. This was quickly joined by strikes from Marine F-4 Phantom IIs. Also coming into play were the 4th Marines and the ARVN 1st Division. An M50A1 Ontos platoon, which had rolled into the area at about 0950, caught the portion of 802nd VC Battalion

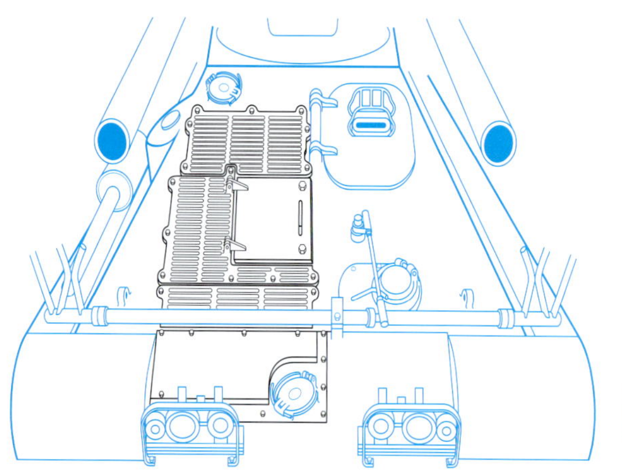

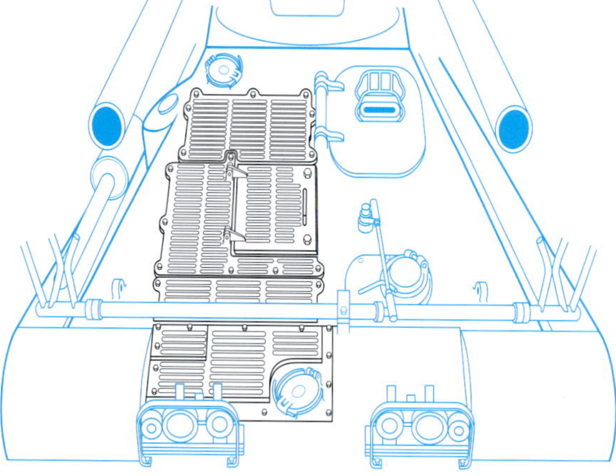

The M50 was powered by a GMC 302 6-cylinder engine. The majority of these vehicles were later repowered with Chrysler V-8 engines, and redesignated M50A1. The configuration of the cooling vents and covers on the glacis changed during this repowering, allowing the M50, *at left*, to be distinguished from the M50A1, shown at right.

west of Route 1 in open ground, obliterating an entire squad with a salvo from the 106 mm rifles.

Significant in the use of Ontos, or any other installation of the M40A1C recoilless rifle, against exposed infantry was the development of the 41-pound M581 antipersonnel-tracer (APERS-T) round, often called beehive. This round contains 1,600 8-grain flechettes and uses four radially spaced detonators for splitting the projectile, while a fifth detonator triggers an expelling charge, which, combined with the centrifugal force of the shell rotation, causes a conical forward dispersion of the flechettes. The round had an effective range of 300 meters. Of course, the M346 high-explosive plastic–tracer (HEP-T) and original fin-stabilized M344 high-explosive, antitank (HEAT) rounds were available as well, the latter of which could penetrate 16 inches of armor at 0 degrees obliquity.

While Ontos was used for convoy escort, improper maintenance caused casualties in this use. Overtightening of the firing cable could allow the firing pin to release unintentionally, thus launching a 106 mm round into friendly vehicles and troops. These instances led to restrictions on the vehicles' use.

Also restricting the use of the vehicles was a chronic shortage of parts. While many vehicles used by the USMC were also in use by the Army, thus permitting the Marines to draw on Army stocks (and depot system), the Ontos (and the Mighty Mite) were USMC-only vehicles, which limited the number of in-theater spare parts. Tracks were particularly in short supply, even as early as April 1966.

On May 18, 1967, 3rd Marine Division units launched Operation Hickory north of Con Thien, an effort to push back the North Vietnamese army (NVA). At 1100 hours they made contact with the enemy, later determined to be two battalions of NVA in well-prepared bunkers and trenches. The Ontos again proved to be an effective antipersonnel weapon.

During December 1967, the 1st and 3rd Antitank Battalions were inactivated, with A Company from each battalion being attached to the constituent tank battalions.

Soon, those Ontos and their crews would be involved in some of the heaviest fighting of the war.

On January 30, 1968, eight battalions of NVA infantry entered Huế, with a division in reserve. To counter this, the Marines sent tank platoons from the 1st and 3rd Tank Battalions, as well as two Ontos platoons of A Company, 3rd Antitank Battalion. With no tanks to fight in Vietnam, the tanks had few armor-piercing projectiles, so the Ontos HEAT rounds were used to open the thick masonry walls as the Marines retook the city building by

An M50A1 undergoes tests for its ability to negotiate a shallow, paved V trench without being damaged or becoming incapacitated. It was important to determine these parameters, as an Ontos that became stuck in a dip or trench could be a dead Ontos. *TACOM LCMC History Office*

building and block by block. It was noted that at 300–500 yards, the M50A1 could open "4 square meter holes or completely knock out an exterior wall."

In addition to being used against NVA infantry, Ontos crews also fired APERS-T rounds at masonry buildings, the cloud of dust being thrown up by the impact serving as a substitute for smoke rounds, allowing Marine infantry to move under cover. The Ontos were not unscathed, however, with three of the vehicles being knocked out and some of their crews lost in the fighting.

In a time frame overlapping the Battle of Huế, another action saw use of the Ontos—the seventy-seven-day battle of Khe Sanh. This battle is notable in being a rare instance of the use of armor by the NVA, which employed four tank battalions equipped with Soviet-built PT-76s. Ten M50A1s of 3rd Antitank Battalion were used for patrol and perimeter defense. Typically the vehicles were hidden during the day, but at night, when the enemy threat was highest, they moved into fighting positions.

In 1969, the Marines began to leave Vietnam. Spare parts for the Ontos were in short supply, and many of the vehicles were well worn. While some were withdrawn with the Marines, others were left behind, turned over to Company D, 16th Armor, 173rd Airborne Brigade, US Army. The company used them until the supply of spare parts was exhausted, then converted them to fixed bunkers.

In 1970, in the US, the Marine 2nd Antitank Battalion was dissolved, and their Ontos turned in. The final unit operating the Ontos attached to the garrison stationed at Guantanamo Bay, Cuba, which kept a solitary M50A1 in operation until 1980.

M50A1 registration number 226712 demonstrates its ability to surmount a vertical obstacle. Trials demonstrated that the M50A1 could negotiate a vertical wall up to 28 feet tall. Further, it could manage a maximum grade of 60 percent and cross a trench up to 4½ feet wide. *TACOM LCMC History Office*

The National Museum of the Marine Corps at Quantico, Virginia, is custodian of this preserved M50A1 Ontos. It is shown here in a re-enactment scenario of street fighting in Vietnam. The Ontos won particular laurels performing infantry support during the close-quarters fighting in the city of Huế during the 1968 Tet Offensive. The louvered engine-access door and transmission cover are hallmarks of the M50A1. These louvered panels were in addition to the upper, center, and lower air-intake louvers, which had also been present on the earlier M50 Ontos. As was typical on operational Ontos, the horn is missing next to the right service headlight. There are rifle shoes with their clamping bands around the number-1 and number-6 recoilless rifle barrels and there is an actuating rod for the travel lock to the front of the driver's hatch. *Author*

Formerly in the collection of the Patton Museum of Cavalry and Armor at Fort Knox, Kentucky, this M50A1 has since been placed in storage following the closure of that museum. Here, the travel lock is lowered, and several of the recoilless rifles are fitted with muzzle covers, complete with the straps used to tie them securely. *Don Moriarty*

All four road wheels are mounted on supporting arms. The two front supporting arms have cutouts in their cross-shafts, into which the rears of the drive sprockets disappear. The outer ends of all the cross-shafts are tapped for eight hex screws, which secure the side channel of the suspension to the supporting arms. *Don Moriarty*

Each of the track assemblies of the M50A1, like those of the M50, was made up of two parallel bands of rubber to which metal crossbars were attached at intervals, forming both the track's treads and the center guides. Two outer guides were also attached to each crossbar on both sides of the center guide. *Don Moriarty*

The cutout in the front of the left front supporting arm gives clearance for the dual sprockets. The profiles of the track crossbars and outer track guides are visible. Locking wires around the hex screws secure the sprocket assembly to the hub. *Don Moriarty*

The rear wheels are mounted on movable supporting arms at the rear of the suspension side channels. Horizontal screws adjacent to the wheel hub on the outside and inside of each supporting arm serve to adjust the track tension. At the upper left is a rubber track skid bumper; these were mounted in pairs above each supporting arm. *Don Moriarty*

Turning the hex head of the outer track-adjusting screw at the rear end of the rear road wheel supporting arm moves the rear road wheel forward or backward, thus adjusting the track tension. The track was to be tensioned so that there was about 2 inches of sag at the center of the top run of the track, give or take a half inch. *Don Moriarty*

This photo gives an idea of the construction of the tracks, with the rubber bands sandwiched between the track crossbars on the outer side of the track, secured with hex-headed cap screws and self-locking hex nuts to reinforcement plates. The inner and outer guides are similarly screwed to the crossbars. *Don Moriarty*

The fenders were fabricated from armor plate bolted to the upper hull. The top surface of the fenders tapered toward the rear of the vehicle. Toward the upper left is the left taillight assembly. The sloping rear of the upper hull is visible in profile to the right. *Don Moriarty*

The left taillight assembly is viewed from below. The feature to the right (i.e., upper rear) of the taillight is the armored cover for the crew compartment blower outlet. The blower is inside the vehicle, directly behind the cover. *Don Moriarty*

Looking at the left taillight assembly from above, the two hex-headed cap screws that fasten the assembly to the hull are visible. A bent steel strip acts as reinforcement between the brush guard and the cable-connectors cover. *Don Moriarty*

To the left, at the forward end of the taillight assembly, is the cable-connectors cover, which protects the electrical wires and connectors from the elements and from potential physical damage. This cover is connected to threaded studs attached to the taillight brush guard with two hex nuts. The taillight housing fits quite tightly within the brush guard. Above the taillight to the upper right is the armored plate assembly that covers the crew compartment blower outlet. There is a small air opening on the side of this cover. The business end of the left taillight, not visible here, includes a service stop lamp at the top and a blackout taillamp at the bottom. *Don Moriarty*

The two U-shaped brackets toward the front of the left side of the upper hull are for stowing a tripod for the .30-caliber machine gun. To the rear of the brackets are spare track crossbars and a 5-gallon liquid container. *Don Moriarty*

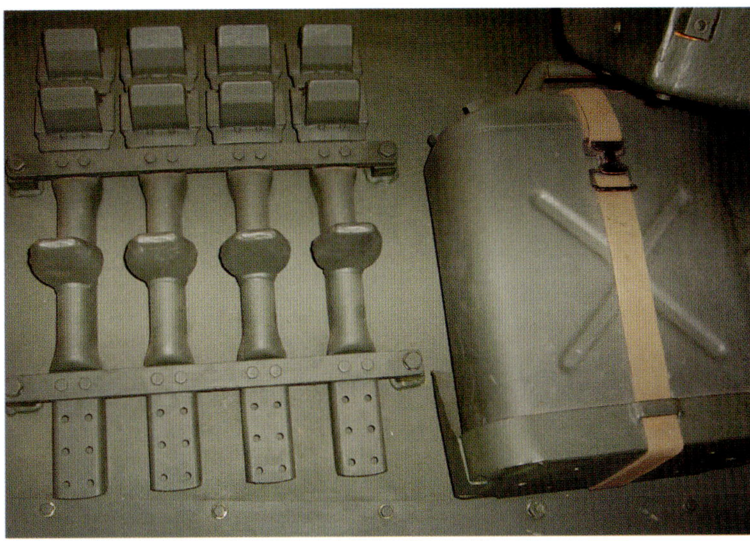

The perforations in the track crossbars are for attaching the outer track guides and the reinforcing plates to the rubber bands. When the crossbars were stowed, it was common practice to attach both outer track guides together on one side of the bars. *Don Moriarty*

There are three brackets for stowing the .30-caliber machine gun tripod, including the triangular one to the left. The machine gun on the turret could be dismounted and placed on the tripod for use away from the vehicle. *Don Moriarty*

A view from the left front of the M50A1 reveals the driver's hatch and periscope mount, the front of the turret, and the cradle for the nos. 1–3 recoilless rifles. The cradles are attached to the cross-shaft that runs through the front of the turret. The gunner's periscope and guard are to the left. *Don Moriarty*

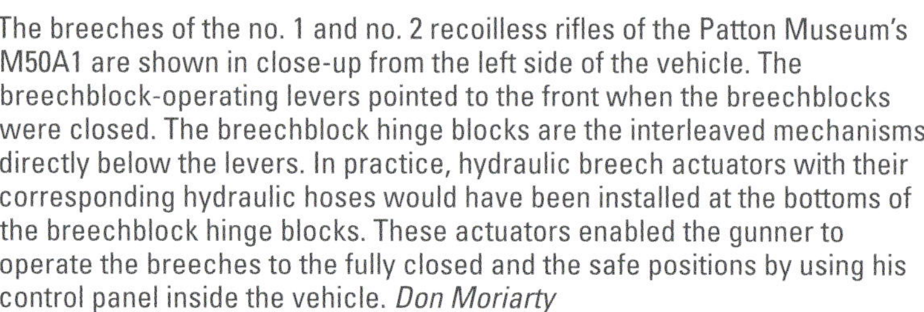

The breeches of the no. 1 and no. 2 recoilless rifles of the Patton Museum's M50A1 are shown in close-up from the left side of the vehicle. The breechblock-operating levers pointed to the front when the breechblocks were closed. The breechblock hinge blocks are the interleaved mechanisms directly below the levers. In practice, hydraulic breech actuators with their corresponding hydraulic hoses would have been installed at the bottoms of the breechblock hinge blocks. These actuators enabled the gunner to operate the breeches to the fully closed and the safe positions by using his control panel inside the vehicle. *Don Moriarty*

The cradles of the no. 1 and no. 2 recoilless rifles are viewed from the left, with the breeches out of view to the right. Quick-release clamps, secured by two T bolts with cross-shaped clamp nuts on each cradle, secure the rifle barrels to the cradles. Projecting from each barrel between the clamps are projectile indicators, which would have been connected with cables to the gunner's panel, signaling which rifles were loaded. At the top is a .50-caliber spotting-rifle receiver and loading port. In front (left) of the cradles are mounts for the M92F elbow telescopes and their covers, used when the recoilless rifles were removed and mounted on tripods for ground firing. *Don Moriarty*

In a view of the underside of the left 106 mm recoilless-rifle cradle assembly, the barrel of the no. 1 rifle is at the upper right. At the lower center, the junction between the left side of the turret and the left cradle is visible. *Don Moriarty*

The no. 2 recoilless rifle's position in the cradle is shown in close-up from slightly to the rear. Toward the top of the photo, locking nuts secure the hinged clamps. The round socket at the rear of the cradle is the receptacle for the breech-actuator line. *Don Moriarty*

The front of the left recoilless-rifle cradle is shown from a different angle. On the left cradle only, a leaf spring was installed on the front of the assembly, with the inboard end of the spring engaging a cylindrical stud projecting from the turret. *Don Moriarty*

Facing the rear of the left recoilless-rifle cradle, the no. 1 rifle is at the bottom and the no. 2 at top. To the left is the elbow telescope mount for the no. 1 rifle, to the right of which is one of the mountings for the .50-caliber spotting rifle associated with the no. 1 recoilless rifle. *Don Moriarty*

Rifle shoes were clamped with two bands to the undersides of the no. 1 and no. 6 recoilless-rifle barrels (the no. 1 rifle is shown here) to serve both as stops for the travel lock and as auxiliary latches to engage with the travel-lock saddles during combat. *Don Moriarty*

Features at the breech end of an M40A1C 106 mm recoilless rifle are exhibited. To the left are the operating lever and the breechblock hinge block. The lateral bar is the breechblock hinge, toward the left of which is the trigger housing. *Don Moriarty*

The rifle shoes are secured with steel clamping bands tightened with two nuts and bolts. During combat, the clamps of the travel locks would be secured open, allowing the driver to freely deploy or disengage the lock, using the rifle shoes as latches. *Don Moriarty*

The rear face of the breech includes four oval vents for expelling propellant gases to the rear. At the center of that face is the breechblock. Around the perimeter of the breech are casting marks, including the weapon's nomenclature information. *Don Moriarty*

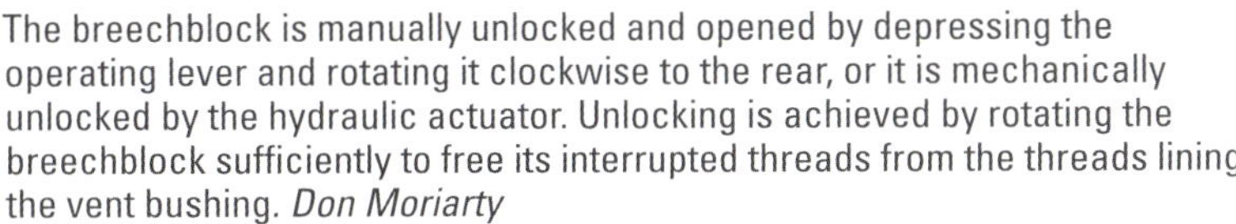

The breechblock is manually unlocked and opened by depressing the operating lever and rotating it clockwise to the rear, or it is mechanically unlocked by the hydraulic actuator. Unlocking is achieved by rotating the breechblock sufficiently to free its interrupted threads from the threads lining the vent bushing. *Don Moriarty*

Within the breechblock hinge is a sliding cocking cam plate; the rotational movement of the breechblock-operating lever moved the cam plate, rotating the breechblock so it can lock or unlock. At the center of the breechblock is the firing pin. *Don Moriarty*

The breech end of the no. 2 recoilless rifle and the open breechblock are seen from the left side. The object on the breechblock hinge with the appearance of a large hex nut is the firing-pin housing cap. *Don Moriarty*

Facing forward from the left rear corner of the M50A1, part of the rear face of the breech of the no. 1 recoilless rifle, including a vent, is at the top left. Below it is the left taillight, which is the standard waterproof "M series" lamp assembly. To the right of the lamp is the armored cover for the fighting-compartment blower vent. *Don Moriarty*

At the lower center of each rear door are hold-open latches, which engage the doorstops when the doors are opened. The doors are released from the stops by pulling a latch knob inside the door. The vision port in the right door is open, but the locking handle on the upper corner of the adjacent door is missing. *Don Moriarty*

The open rear doors of the M50A1 reveal the interior of the crew compartment, with the gunner's seat at the center and the driver's seat at the far left corner. Below the door, the elongated door of the 106 mm ammunition stowage compartment is open, showing the bases of six of the eight rounds, the other two being on display. *Don Moriarty*

In this left rear three-quarters view of an M50A1, the recoilless rifles are secured in their travel locks and the rear doors are secured. The frames on either side of the rear doors of the crew compartment are the doorstops. Above the doors are the radio mast and its mount. *Don Moriarty*

The 106 mm shell stowage compartment comprises eight steel tubes protected by an armored door. To release a round, its shell fastener was turned out of the way, and a spring partially ejected the round from its tube. Two handles inside the rear of the crew compartment operated the door's latches.

Inside the left rear door of the M50A1 are two latch handles. Only the upper handle had an attached external handle. Once both doors were closed, the left door was latched; a flange on the edge of the door held the right door shut. For weatherproofing, rubber seals were fitted around the edge of the door opening and on the joint where the two doors met. Toward the lower center of the left door is the doorstop latch release button. The cylinder attached to the top of the lower hinge houses a torsion spring to assist in opening and closing the door. Below the door is the left mud flap. *Don Moriarty*

The right door has a vision port with a sliding armored panel on the inside. On the lower rear of the hull below each lower hinge of the doors are a towing lug and shackle. Above the center of the rear of the hull are the radio antenna and its mounting bracket, with the insulator and antenna lead-in cable visible. In this photo, the shell stowage compartment door is shut. The small protrusion above the top edge of this door, virtually straight down from the rear door hold-open latch, is the latch for the shell stowage compartment door. There is a similar latch on the opposite side of the top of the door. *Don Moriarty*

The latch on the upper left edge of the shell stowage compartment door is visible below the left rear hull door. It is simply a shaft with an oblong piece mounted off-center on the end, such that when the latch handle inside the crew compartment is turned, the oblong piece engages a D-shaped recess in the top of the shell stowage compartment door, holding it shut. Welded to the upper part of that door to the left of center is a grab handle, fabricated from a piece of bent steel rod. The hold-open latch on the rear door and the left doorstop are visible in profile. Toward the top is the housing for the counterbalance spring. *Don Moriarty*

Looking toward the right rear of the upper hull of an M50A1 (*right*) and the open right door (*left*), the sprung hold-open latch is seen engaged to the doorstop. The actuating rod connected to the release button can be seen coming through the door. *Don Moriarty*

There is no grab handle on the right side of the shell stowage compartment door. Details of the right rear fender and the doorstop are visible. Below that door, its right hinge is visible. Attached to the rear of the fender is a rubber mud flap with a metal retainer strip across its top. Leaking lubricants have stained the inside of the rear road wheel, a common occurrence on the Ontos and other tracked vehicles. Around the perimeter of the tracks, the outer guides are arranged, with one attached to each track crossbar. On the near side of the wheel hub is the hex head of the inner adjusting screw for the rear wheel.

Part of the rear of the crew compartment appears through the open right door (its edge running up and down the center of the photo). On the inside of the bottom of the doorway, the latch handles for the ammunition compartment door are visible. *Don Moriarty*

At the top of the interior of the right rear door of an M50A1 is the sliding armored panel for the vision port. Below the vision port is a compartmentalized stowage box designed to hold four smoke canister grenades. *Don Moriarty*

The smoke grenade box is shown with its lid open. Earlier, on the M50 Ontos, in this location was mounted a simple holder for the primer protectors, capable of holding two stacks of the devices side by side. *Don Moriarty*

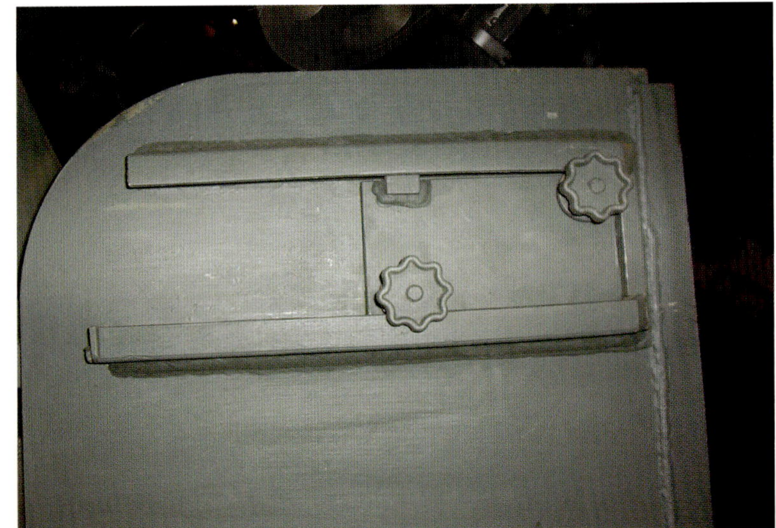

The sliding panel of the right door's vision port fits within upper and lower tracks welded to the interior of the door. The knurled knobs are turned to lock the panel in place. The flange on the edge of the door is welded in place. *Don Moriarty*

The entire breadth of the shell compartment door, with its off-center grab handle, locking latches, and hinges, is displayed. Inside the crew compartment are the rack for four rounds of 106 mm ammunition (*right*) and the rear of the gunner's seat. *Don Moriarty*

The Ontos fired this M344 high-explosive antitank round. The projectile was painted Olive Drab, with yellow stenciling indicating the model and type of cartridge and projectile, as well as the caliber and type of weapon with which it was to be used. On the base of the round, in white, was stenciled the ammunition lot number, the model of cartridge, and the model of weapon. The complete round measured 39.31 inches long. Other types of ammunition, similar in appearance, were also used, including the M346 high-explosive plastic–tracer (HEP-T) and the antipersonnel—also known as beehive—round, containing six thousand 13-grain flechettes.

	M50	M50A1
Combat weight	19,050 pounds	19,130 pounds
Height	83.9 inches	83.9 inches
Length	150.8 inches	150.8 inches
Width over fenders	102.3 inches	102.3 inches
Tread	73.0 inches	73.0 inches
Ground clearance	14.6 inches	14.6 inches
Powerplant	General Motors Model 302: 6 cylinder, gasoline	Chrysler HT-361-318: V-8 gasoline
Horsepower, Gross	145 @ 3,400 rpm	180 @ 3,450 rpm
Torque, Gross	255 ft.-lb. at 2,000 rpm	283 ft.-lb. at 2,400 rpm
Transmission	Allison Crossdrive XT-90-2 3 forward, 1 reverse	Allison Crossdrive XT-90-5 3 forward, 1 reverse
Fuel capacity	47 gallons	47 gallons
Performance		
Max level road speed	30 mph	30 mph
Max trench	54 inches	54 inches
Max grade	60 percent grade	60 percent grade
Max vertical obstacle	28 inches	28 inches
Min turning diameter	18 feet	18 feet
Max fording depth	24 inches	24 inches
Cruising range	~115 miles, roads	~100 miles, roads
Armament		
Primary	Six 106 mm Recoilless Rifles M40A1C T149E5 on turret	
Traverse	80° (40° left and right; manual)	
Elevation	+20° to -10° (manual)	
Ammo Stowage	18 rounds	
Secondary	.30 cal. M1919A4 MG fixed or flexible in turret mount	
Ammo stowage	1,000 rounds	
Fire height, top rifles	about 78 inches	
Turret ring diameter	31.7 inches	

The ammunition rack in the crew compartment consists of a hinged, removable shell-supporting plate (below the fire extinguisher) and the clamp frame (*foreground*). The sequence of photographs on the next two pages shows how the ammunition rounds were loaded in the rack. *Don Moriarty*

Two 106 mm rounds are resting in the rack. The shell-supporting plate is removable and when not in use was folded to the rear to rest against the side of the hull. The clamp frame was removable and was secured in place with retaining pins. *Don Moriarty*

The holes in the shell-supporting plate hold the projectile ends of the shells. Black cushioning material surrounded the holes (this material is missing from the lower right hole). The opposite end of the shell rests in a cradle. *Don Moriarty*

The center clamp has been lowered over the two 106 mm casings. The top side of this clamp forms the cradle for the two upper rounds, not yet emplaced. The small round objects on the cradle are rubber bumpers. *Don Moriarty*

The two upper rounds are now in the rack. The smaller hole in the shell-supporting plate for the upper right round makes that round sit farther back; this was necessary because of the angle of the engine compartment bulkhead to the front. *Don Moriarty*

The final step in loading the ammunition rack was to lower and secure the top clamp over the upper two rounds. On the hull above and right of the clamp is the panel for the battery compartment, holding two Delco-Remy 6TN 12-volt batteries. *Don Moriarty*

The gunner's seat has a fixed backrest with binoculars holder on the back and a vertically adjustable bucket seat. To its front are the weapons control panel, elevation handwheel with red grip, radio, driver's seat, and, to the right, engine compartment. *Don Moriarty*

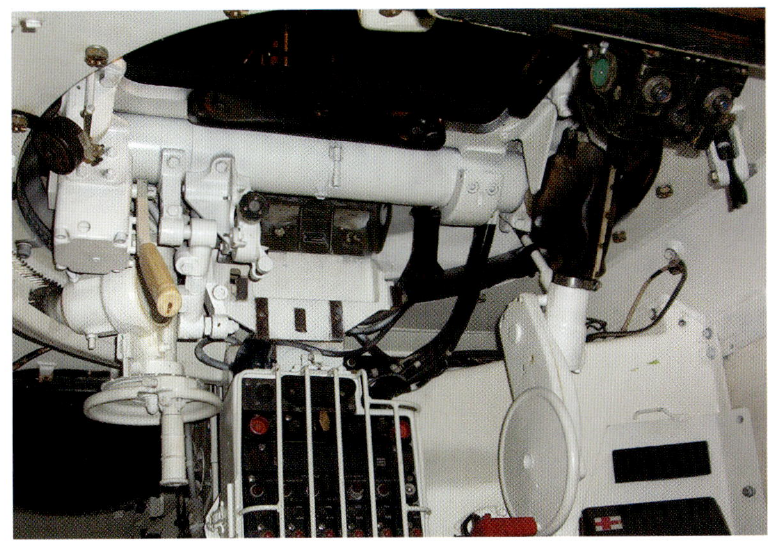

In this gunner's view of the turret interior, the weapons-control panel at center is flanked by the traverse handwheel (*at left*) and the elevation handwheel (*at right*). Overhead are the hatch, the cross-shaft of the weapons mount, and the periscope mount. *Don Moriarty*

Inside the upper left side of the rear door is the ventilator blower. Below it is the box for .50-caliber spotter-tracer ammunition. Footman loops for strapping down .30-caliber ammunition boxes are on the fender. *Author*

Fitted with a protective cage, the weapons control panel allowed the gunner to monitor which recoilless rifles were loaded and on safe; to arm, select, and fire the spotting rifles; to select or fire the recoilless rifles; and to perform other functions. *Don Moriarty*

The door of the .50-caliber ammunition box is open, showing the racks inside for holding four magazines. Each magazine holds twenty rounds. This type of spotting ammunition included a tracer that emitted a flash and puff of smoke when it impacted. *Don Moriarty*

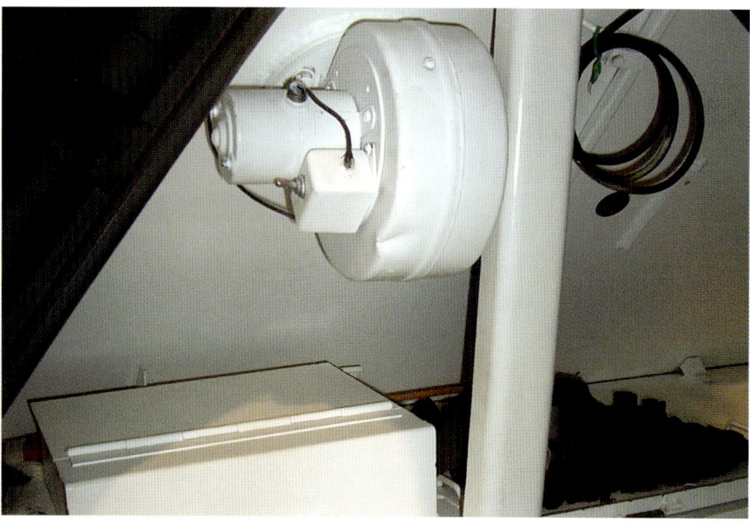

This view shows the left rear area of the crew compartment aboard a different M50A1 from that seen on page 67. Here, a hand grenade box is stored below the .50-caliber ammunition box. The blower served to exhaust air from the crew compartment through the covered vent on the left rear of the upper hull. The blower switch is on the side of the unit; on the opposite side of the blower is the air inlet, protected by a metal screen. The stanchions in the crew compartment acted to support and strengthen the hull roof, which carried the considerable weight of the recoilless rifles and their mount, as well as the cast-steel turret, rifle cradles, and weapons control panel. *Don Moriarty*

The left rear side of the crew compartment is viewed from the driver's compartment. In the foreground is the radio rack, while toward the upper rear of the compartment is the front side of the blower, with the inlet screen visible. *Don Moriarty*

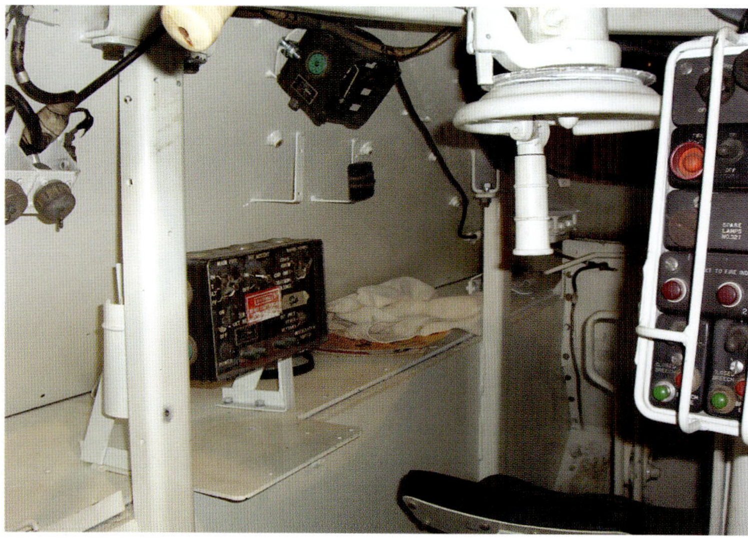

In the left sponson of the M50A1 was an AN/PRC-10 radio set, comprising an RT-175/PRC-19 receiver-transmitter and AM-598U amplifier. Here, just an audio amplifier is mounted on the fender. Above it is an intercom control box. *Don Moriarty*

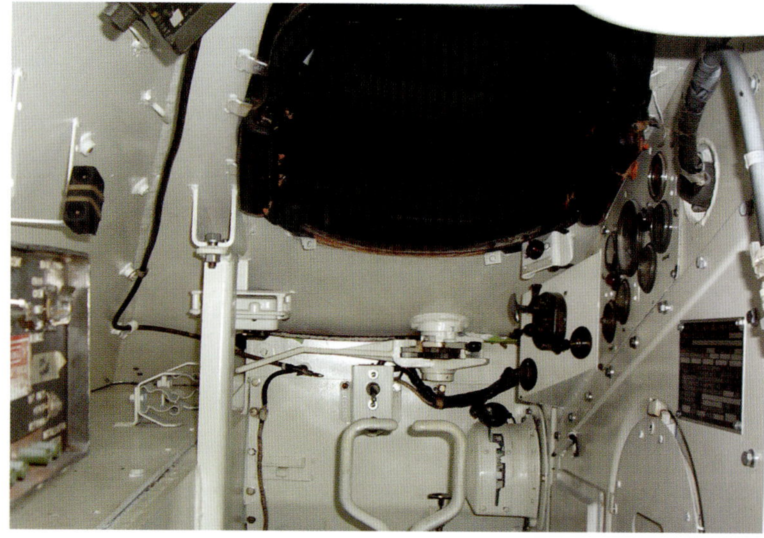

The driver's compartment of an M50A1 is viewed facing toward the front. Above is the hatch cover and to the lower left of it is the forward stanchion. The steering-brake control levers are below the hatch, with the instrument panel to the right. *Don Moriarty*

The master switch and indicator light are located to the front of the driver's compartment. Above them is the recoilless-rifle travel lock control. To the lower right is the manual shifting and starting lever. *Don Moriarty*

To the driver's right is the instrument panel, below which is the engine partition, with the vehicle's nomenclature and data plate to the right. The oval door provided access to the engine compartment and also was used for ventilation purposes. *Don Moriarty*

The adjustable seat back and its locking handle are visible in this view of the driver's seat, as seen looking down through the driver's hatch. The seat could be raised to five positions, with a maximum vertical rise of 6¾ inches, using a lever under the left side of the seat. There is a brass grommet on the covering of the seat cushion. To the left of the seat is the rear corner of the engine partition. The floor exhibits considerable pitting, a result of decades of exposure to the elements and corrosion. At the top of the photo (behind the driver's seat) is a floor-mounted radio transmitter-receiver.

To the front of the driver's seat and steering brake levers are, *left to right*, the footrest with headlight dimmer switch, periscope storage box, and accelerator pedal. On the partition to the right of the steering levers is a cover over what had been the engine partition door. *Don Moriarty*

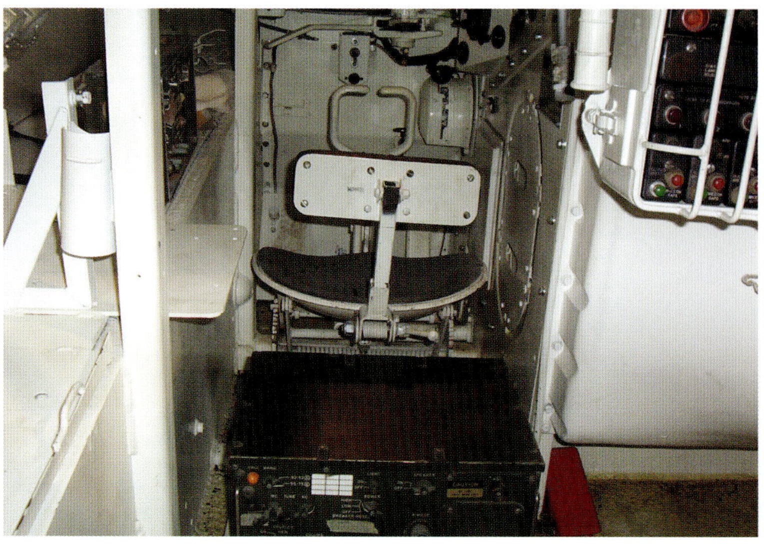

The driver's compartment is viewed from the rear. At the bottom is a floor-mounted RT-524/VRC FM transmitter-receiver. To the upper right is the weapons control panel, and below it is the rear bulkhead of the engine compartment. *Don Moriarty*

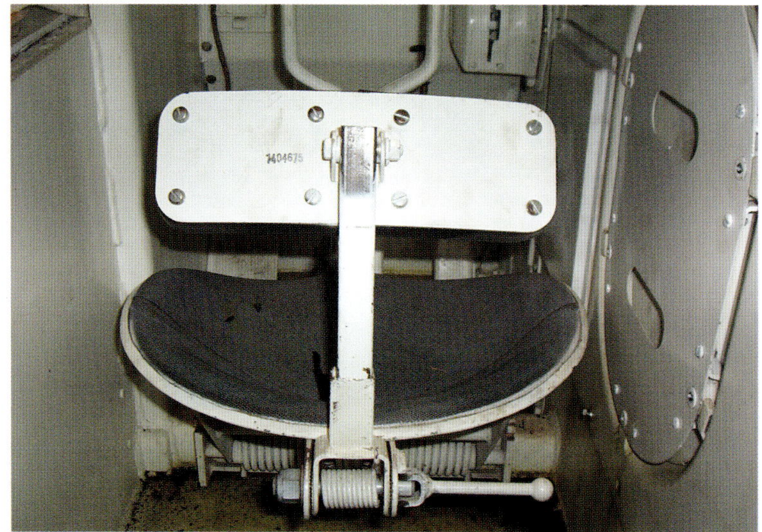

The driver's seat back could be adjusted from full vertical to full horizontal by using the lever to the right rear of the seat. The seat was mounted on a support bracket fastened to the floor. Both seat and seat back had cushions. *Don Moriarty*

The gunner's seat is viewed from the left rear. The seat support is bolted to the structural cross-member on the floor. On the back of the seat support is a holder for a pair of binoculars. The holder is fitted with a slot and a footman loop for attaching a retainer strap. *Don Moriarty*

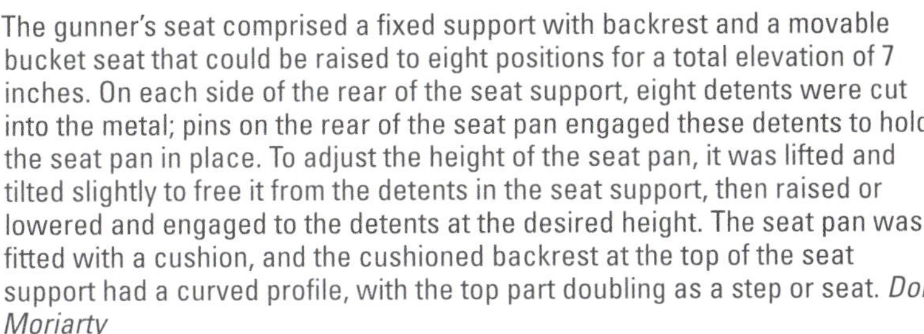

The gunner's seat comprised a fixed support with backrest and a movable bucket seat that could be raised to eight positions for a total elevation of 7 inches. On each side of the rear of the seat support, eight detents were cut into the metal; pins on the rear of the seat pan engaged these detents to hold the seat pan in place. To adjust the height of the seat pan, it was lifted and tilted slightly to free it from the detents in the seat support, then raised or lowered and engaged to the detents at the desired height. The seat pan was fitted with a cushion, and the cushioned backrest at the top of the seat support had a curved profile, with the top part doubling as a step or seat. *Don Moriarty*

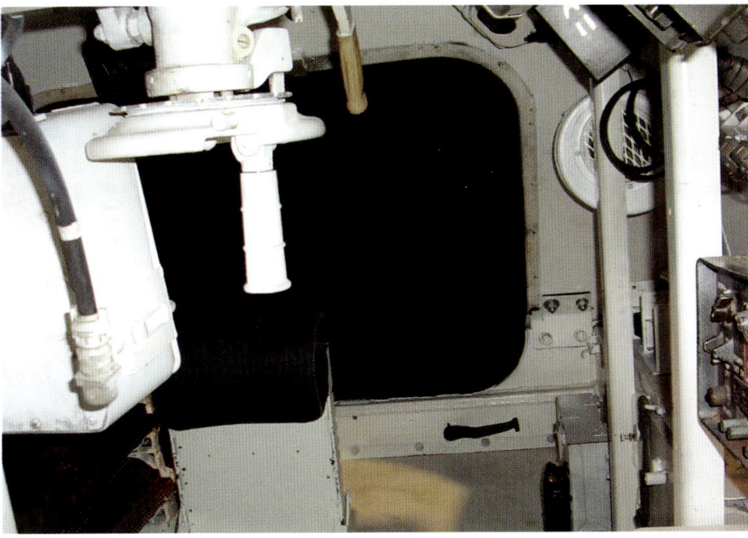

Looking aft from the driver's compartment, above the gunner's seat is the traverse handwheel of the turret. The lever with the grip to the right of the handwheel operated the manual pump for the hydraulic breech-operating mechanism. *Don Moriarty*

The contours of the gunner's bucket seat are visible. At the center of the seat pan cushion is a grommet. Details of the seat pan frame and the detents in the rear of the seat support are also in view. *Don Moriarty*

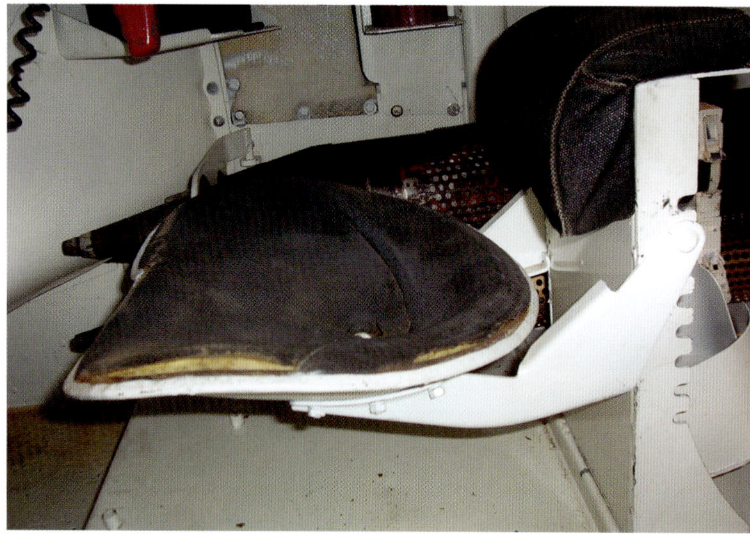

This view of the left side of the gunner's seat shows how the seat pan is fastened to its frame with three cap screws, flat washers, and locking nuts. The same pattern is repeated on the right frame. Beyond the seat is 106 mm ammunition. *Don Moriarty*

The gunner's backrest and seat cushion are shown close-up. The seat support was attached to the channel running across the floor with four hex-headed ⅜-inch cap screws, flat washers, and locking nuts. *Don Moriarty*

The slave receptacle on the right rear of the upper hull was used to transmit external power into the vehicle, for recharging the batteries or starting the vehicle when the batteries' charges were low. The procedure for jump-starting a dead Ontos was to drive a "donor" vehicle as close as possible to it and turn off its engine, turn off the master switches in both vehicles, remove the twist-on covers from the slave receptacles of both vehicles and connect a slave cable into both receptacles, turn on the master switches, and start the dead vehicle's engine. After the slave cable was removed from the receptacles, the Ontos would run its engines to recharge the batteries. *Don Moriarty*

A three-quarters view illustrates the layout of the right rear corner of the Patton Museum's M50A1. To the right of the doorstop is the slave receptacle, and the right taillight is visible on the side of the hull. *Don Moriarty*

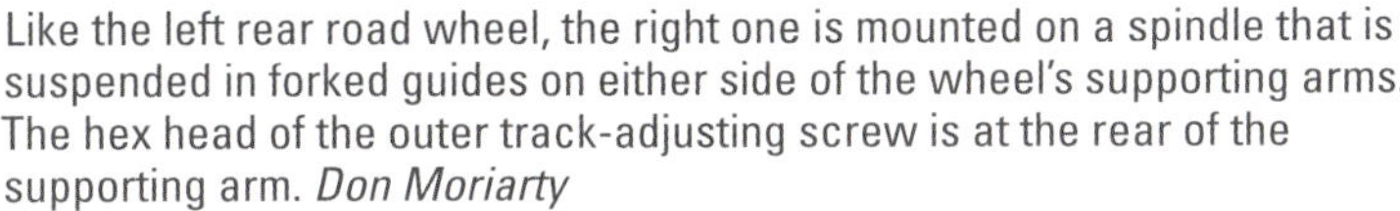
Like the left rear road wheel, the right one is mounted on a spindle that is suspended in forked guides on either side of the wheel's supporting arms. The hex head of the outer track-adjusting screw is at the rear of the supporting arm. *Don Moriarty*

Several of the interleaved bogie wheels are depicted. Each wheel has twenty-four hex bolts around the rim, for attaching the tire-retainer ring, located on the reverse side of the wheel. The tires were vulcanized rubber, with steel wire embedded in them for extra strength. Square-pattern Zimmerit is on the side of the hull. *Author*

Bolted underneath the fenders on both sides of the vehicle are wooden track upper skids, which, along with the track bumper skids, acted to limit the vertical travel of the upper tracks. Also visible are the right rear fender and mud flap. *Don Moriarty*

This view of the breech ends of the no, 5 and no. 6 recoilless rifles shows the firing cables attached to the pieces. Atop the no. 5 recoilless rifle is the receiver of the spotting rifle. Underneath the rifles is the pioneer tool rack. *Don Moriarty*

From the side, the right cradle of the recoilless guns is similar in appearance to the left cradle, with its quick-release clamps. On the underside of each step in the cradle below the recoilless-rifle tubes, not visible in this photo, are the firing solenoids. At the top is the spotting rifle on the no. 5 recoilless rifle. On the side of the receiver is the charging handle, and coming up to the rear of the receiver is the firing cable. Spotting rifles were mounted over the no. 2 to no. 5 recoilless rifles. Only the spotting rifles over the no. 3 and no. 4 mounts could be fired by the gunner from inside the vehicle. The spotting rifles on the no. 2 and no. 5 recoilless rifles were intended for use when those weapons were dismounted and mounted on tripods. *Don Moriarty*

A .50-caliber spotting rifle is installed above the no. 5 recoilless rifle in the right cradle of this display M50A1. The .50-caliber rifle was a gas-operated semiautomatic weapon; alongside its barrel is the gas cylinder assembly. *Don Moriarty*

The pioneer rack holds an ax, shovel, mattock head, and handle. Clips, brackets, and buckled webbing strips secure the tools in place. On the underside of the cradle to the far left is a hole from which the firing solenoid has been removed. *Don Moriarty*

On the right side of the upper hull is the pioneer tool rack. Below the rack is the right taillight assembly, incorporating a blackout stop lamp over a blackout taillamp. To the bottom right are the tailpipe and muffler. *Don Moriarty*

From left to right: the tail pipe, muffler, and exhaust pipe. Below the fender, details of the tracks are visible. The hex-headed cap screws on the track crossbars were notoriously susceptible to erosion during protracted operations on sand and gravel. *Don Moriarty*

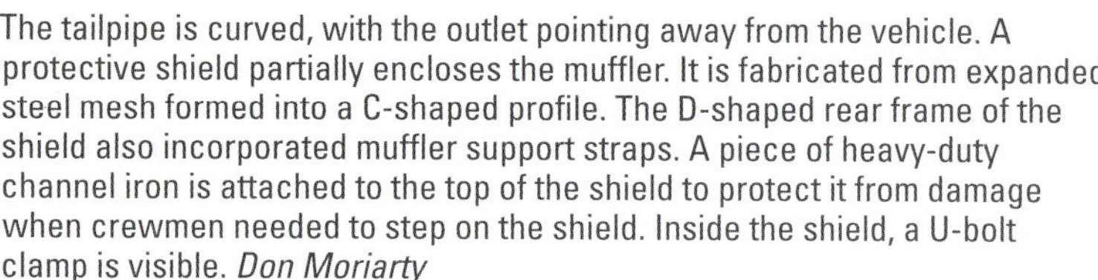

The tailpipe is curved, with the outlet pointing away from the vehicle. A protective shield partially encloses the muffler. It is fabricated from expanded steel mesh formed into a C-shaped profile. The D-shaped rear frame of the shield also incorporated muffler support straps. A piece of heavy-duty channel iron is attached to the top of the shield to protect it from damage when crewmen needed to step on the shield. Inside the shield, a U-bolt clamp is visible. *Don Moriarty*

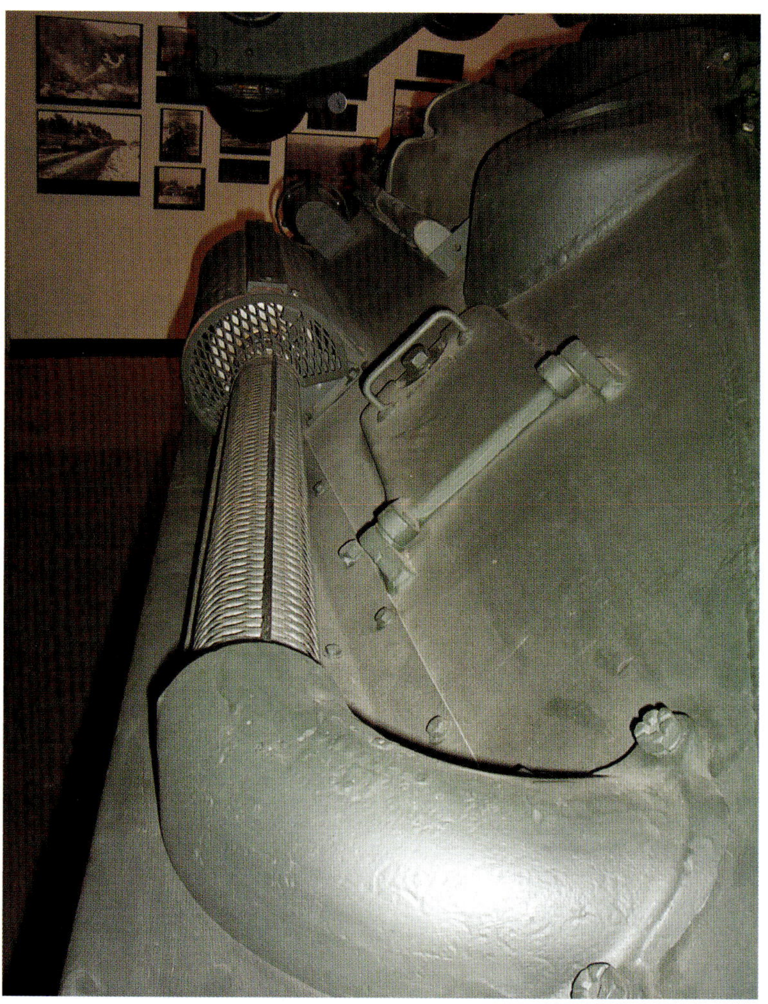

Looking toward the rear from the right front of the M50A1, the exhaust pipe elbow is in the foreground. On this example of an Ontos, the exhaust pipe has its own shield of expanded steel mesh. The door at the center of the photograph provided access to the oil-bath air cleaner inside the engine compartment. The Ontos operator's manual referred to the part of the fender shown here, between the front and rear faces of the hull, as the outer intermediate fender. *Don Moriarty*

The exhaust line, shield, and elbow are viewed from the side. Above the exhaust line, the air cleaner service door has a grab handle and a latch bolt. During active operations it was necessary to replenish the oil in the air cleaner daily. *Don Moriarty*

The exhaust pipe elbow was attached to the side of the hull with three hex-headed cap screws and lock washers. Faintly visible on the top of the elbow, a foundry mark and part number are cast into the surface. *Don Moriarty*

The shield of the muffler is viewed from the front end. In addition to protecting the exhaust elements from physical damage, the shields protected crewmen from burns should they accidentally brush against the parts while the engine was running. *Don Moriarty*

The exhaust elbow is viewed from the rear. At the top of the photo is the right side of the crossbar of the travel lock. The joint between the side of the upper hull and the glacis is welded. *Don Moriarty*

Seen from above is the bulged casting welded to the right side of the hull to accommodate the air cleaner. The part number is cast on its top surface. Also on the top is the removable plug for the snorkel that was part of the deepwater-fording kit. *Don Moriarty*

The bulge over the air cleaner is viewed here from the rear, with the shovel in the pioneer tool rack appearing in the foreground. The plug for the snorkel opening has a built-in handle and is removed by twisting and pulling it. *Don Moriarty*

The bulged casting over the oil-bath air cleaner is viewed from the front right side of the M50A1. To the rear of the casting is the pioneer tool rack, while on the glacis to the side of the casting is the access cover for the radiator filler opening. *Don Moriarty*

The front right side of the hull of another M50A1 is seen here, with the air cleaner service door at the bottom. This door is hinged to two lugs welded to the hull. To the right are the center and rear air-intake louvers. *Author*

The air cleaner service door is open, showing its raised rim and its D-shaped latch on its inner surface. The door was hung on the hinges with 0.625" × 1.75" headed-type hinge pins secured in place with spring pins. *Don Moriarty*

The upper eyebolt pertains to the lower of two clamping bands that support the air cleaner. To the right is the generator, a belt-driven, fully enclosed, watertight, four-pole shunt-type unit. *Don Moriarty*

The oil cup of the air cleaner is at the left in this view inside the open air cleaner service door. Turning the eyebolt next to the oil cup loosens a clamp band, allowing the cup to be removed for cleaning and refilling.

The travel lock is seen supporting the no. 6 recoilless-rifle barrel on this M50A1 draped with camouflage netting. The barrel rests in the saddle, and the locking lever and clamp hook hold the top clamp in place. Below the saddle is a rubber bumper. *Author*

This frontal view of the M50A1 at the Patton Museum shows the louvered engine-access and transmission-access doors that were introduced with that model of the Ontos. It is evident that the driver's compartment took up less than half the width of the hull. *Don Moriarty*

The engine access door (*lower right*), though small, provided ready access to the engine oil filler cap and other components inside the engine compartment. More mechanisms could be accessed by unbolting and removing the other louvers. To the right is the driver's hatch and door.

The small size of the crew compartment roof of the Ontos, most of which is occupied by the correspondingly small turret, is apparent in this overhead view. Regulation muzzle covers are fitted over the no. 3 and no. 4 recoilless rifles. The thinness of the barrel walls is also visible. *Don Moriarty*

The features of the right side of the travel lock are displayed. On the outboard side of the saddle are the locking lever and the red-painted hook that holds the top clamp secure. When the barrel is resting in the lock, the barrel shoe fits into the square opening below the saddle. *Don Moriarty*

On the front right side of the glacis of the Patton Museum's M50A1 is the right headlight array. To the left in the photo is the blackout marker light, next to which is the service headlight. The horn is missing from its mount on the inboard side of the service headlight. All three of these components were mounted on the bracket screwed to the glacis. The service and blackout headlights, blackout marker lights, horn, and taillights all were powered by the batteries. Above the lights is the brush guard, with three braces extending back to a common mounting on the transmission cover. *Don Moriarty*

The left-side array also includes a service headlight (*center*) and blackout marker light (*right*), but it also has a blackout driving light (*left*). The service headlights are secured to their mounting brackets with a mounting nut, lock washer, and bevel washer. Below the lights on both sides of the M50A1 are towing lugs fitted with shackles secured with pins. The bottoms of the front legs of the brush guards are bent to form mounting flanges and are fastened to the glacis with hex screws. The glacis fits on top of the front armored plate of the lower hull, with its front edge exposed. *Don Moriarty*

The bracket for the lights and horn is a piece of channel steel with holes for mounting the fixtures. It is attached to the glacis with nuts and screws. The brush guard brace is fastened to the center of the transmission cover. *Don Moriarty*

The electrical wires and connections of the lights lacked protective conduits and were fully exposed for several inches between the glacis and the light housings. The mount of each service headlight had a shockproof rubber insulator. *Don Moriarty*

The brush guard's construction is of bent and welded metal strips. The center brace is welded under the hoop of the guard, while the two outer braces are welded to the top of the hoop. *Don Moriarty*

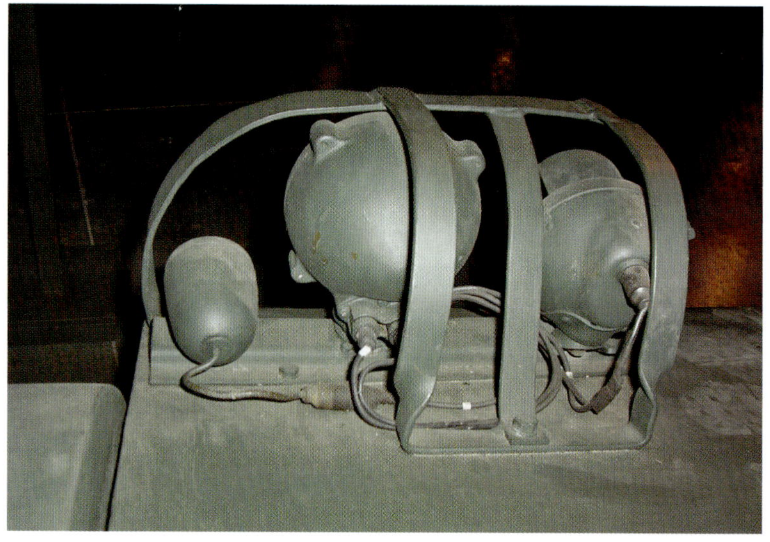

The left service headlight and blackout driving headlight have quick-release electrical connections at the rear of their housings. Coming out of the rear of the housing of the blackout marker light is an electrical lead with a connector. *Don Moriarty*

A straight-on view of the track below the left front fender provides a close-up look at the numerous cap screws that held the tracks together. In the gaps at the center of the track, the two sprockets are visible. *Don Moriarty*

On both sides of the cross-shaft of the travel lock is a mounting bracket that incorporates a shaft bearing; this is the right one. On the far side of the bracket is the right front lifting eye. *Don Moriarty*

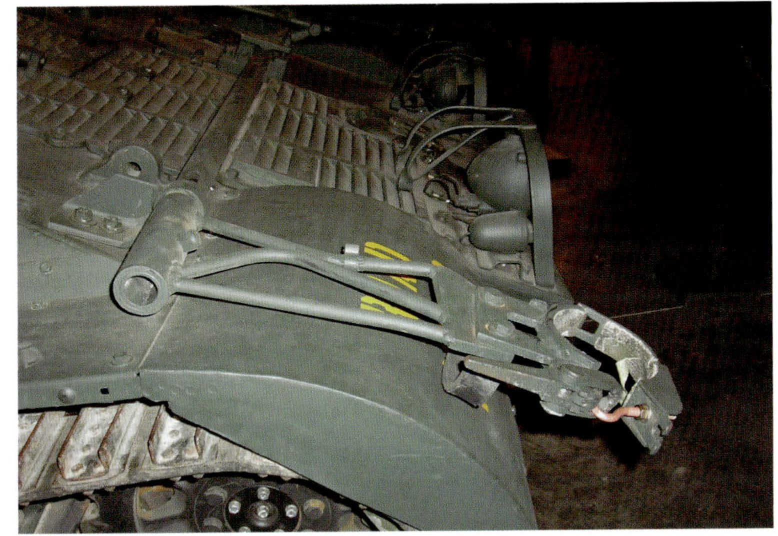

The rubber bumpers of the travel lock form buffers between the lock and the fender. The same cap screws and nuts that fasten the saddles to the tops of the supports also hold the bumpers in place. *Don Moriarty*

Linings were fastened to the inner surfaces of the saddle and top clamp, for cushioning the recoilless-rifle barrels. These linings were fastened with 9/64" × ½" countersunk-head tubular rivets. *Don Moriarty*

Pinned to each of the clamp-locking handles (*lower right*) of the travel lock is a clamp-locking hoop. When the locking handle is engaged, this hoop catches the red clamp hook and draws the top clamp tight over the barrel. *Don Moriarty*

Toward the center of the travel lock cross-shaft is the cross-shaft clamp assembly. Just beyond that assembly is the cross-shaft operating-lever yoke, connected with a ball joint to the control rod leading back to the ratchet shaft arm (*left*). *Don Moriarty*

To raise and lower the travel lock, seen here from the front of the Ontos, the driver operated a ratchet handle inside his compartment. This procedure translated movement through the ratchet shaft arm (in the upper part of the photo) through the control rod to the cross-shaft yoke at the lower center, thus lifting or lowering the travel lock. The oval plate at the center is the fuel pump cover, which also incorporates the fuel tank filler cap cover. The bent rod locks the filler cap cover to a lug on the fuel pump cover. Note the casting number on the transmission cover to the lower left. *Don Moriarty*

With the fuel tank filler cap cover open, the fuel filler cap is visible. Removing the fuel pump cover provided access to the fuel pump and hanger assembly, fuel pump capacitor housing, and the fuel-level indicator transmitter. *Don Moriarty*

The travel lock is shown deployed with the top clamp disengaged. In combat, when the top clamps were left disengaged for quickly raising or lowering of the travel lock, a sprung clamp hold-down handle, not shown here, kept the clamp from flapping around. *Don Moriarty*

When installed, the clamp hold-down handle would have been connected to a clasp on the top clamp (to the left of the red clamp hook) and to a ring clasp on the inboard leg of the travel lock support (the remnant of the ring is visible at the center of the photo). In combat, when the top clamps were left open for rapid deployment or lowering of the travel lock, the barrel shoes would have served the purpose of locking the no. 1 and no. 6 recoilless-rifle barrels to the saddles of the travel locks. The left barrel shoe protrudes through the opening above the rubber bumper. *Don Moriarty*

The left side of the travel lock is seen from the rear. The lining of the saddle is somewhat worn from use, but the lining of the top clamp is in better shape. These linings were fastened with tubular rivets with sunken heads. Six rivets are visible on the lining of the top clamp. To the lower right of the red clamp hook is the clasp for the clamp hold-down handle. The legs of the travel lock support are welded to a horizontal tube that fits over the cross-shaft and is secured with a ½" × 3" hex-headed bolt through a ½" hex-headed nut; the nut is visible at the center of the tube. *Don Moriarty*

As seen from the right front corner of the M50A1, the top clamp of the travel lock is engaged to the clamp-locking hoop. On the support leg to the lower right of the rubber bumper, the ring clasp for the clamp hold-down handle is protruding. *Don Moriarty*

The right travel lock is shown from the rear, clamped to the no. 6 106 mm recoilless-rifle barrel of an M50A1. On the upper surface of the barrel shoe, a lining is present for cushioning purposes. *Don Moriarty*

The transmission cover is on the glacis at the front right corner of the M50A1. This louvered cover replaced a plain armored cover on the M50. On the lower right corner of the cover is the armored cover for the transmission oil filler. *Don Moriarty*

The hinged engine access door is open, exhibiting the depth of its ventilating louvers. Components of the engine are visible within the hull, and to the upper right is the driver's hatch cover. The front of the turret is to the top of the photo. *Don Moriarty*

Parts of the Chrysler HT-361-318 engine and its components are visible through the open engine access door. This eight-cylinder, four-cycle engine had a displacement of 360.9 cubic inches and weighed 710 pounds. It was fed from a fuel tank to the front of the driver's compartment with a capacity of 47 gallons of 80-octane gasoline. Engine oil capacity was 7 quarts. The cramped arrangement of the engine compartment is evident in this photo. On the left are the carburetor, air hose, and throttle linkages. At the upper center is the distributor and ignition and cables. Toward the bottom right is the engine crankcase oil filler and cap. *Don Moriarty*

The seat and steering-brake levers are seen from above, through the driver's hatch. Around the hatch rim are a crash pad and weather seal, and a welded splash guard partly surrounds the opening to deflect projectiles from the closed hatch. *Don Moriarty*

The turret forms the center of the T149E5 106 mm recoilless-rifle mount. Rising above it on a tubular mount is the .30-caliber machine gun. The cradle of the gun could be raised for manual firing. It was lowered for coaxial firing. *Don Moriarty*

The interior of the driver's hatch cover is painted the same color as the exterior of the vehicle. It is fitted with a grab handle, a latch handle with coil spring, and a 360-degree rotating mount for the driver's M13 periscope (not installed). *Don Moriarty*

The machine gun is shown in the raised position. To the rear of it is the gunner's hatch cover with its two interior latch handles and hold-open rod. The objective of the gunner's M20A3G periscope is visible at the front of the turret. *Don Moriarty*

A black crash pad is fastened to the inside of the gunner's hatch cover. To the right is the spotting rifle atop the no. 3 recoilless rifle, along with a .50-caliber ammunition magazine and the bracket for the elbow telescope. *Don Moriarty*

Casting numbers are on top of the periscope shield and the turret. The machine gun as originally configured would have had a firing solenoid, and an elevating and traversing mechanism would have been installed at the rear of the mount. *Don Moriarty*

The magazines for the no. 3 and no. 4 recoilless spotting rifles flank the gunner's hatch. Through the hatch, the red handle of the elevation handwheel is visible. To the rear of the turret is the radio antenna, insulator, and dual-antenna mount.

On top of the cradle between the no. 2 and no. 3 recoilless rifles, the circular plate is the cradle access opening cover. A junction box is attached to the interior side of the cover. On either side are the receivers of the .50-caliber spotting rifles. *Don Moriarty*

On the National Museum of the Marine Corps' M50A1, the travel lock is lowered, showing how the rubber bumpers under the saddles cushion and support the lock when it is lowered onto the front fenders. Also evident are the angles of the front of the hull, with sloping facets designed to multiply the stopping power of the thin, ½-inch-thick armor. The glacis was angled at 71 degrees from vertical, while the lower front of the hull was 45 degrees from vertical. The upper sides of the hull were 42 degrees, while the sides of the lower hull were vertical. The floor of the hull was only ¼ inch thick and thus was very vulnerable to land mines. The cast turret was also ½ inch in thickness. *Author*

From the side, the M50A1 appears the same as the M50. This example has spare track crossbars, each of which included a center track guide, stowed in brackets on the side of the hull. The driver's hatch, hinged to the right side, is open. *Patton Museum*

In a view of the same M50A1 as in the photograph at top, the track skid bumpers mounted between each road wheel are seen to good advantage. Spare track sections are draped over the glacis, and the recoilless rifles are well covered. *Patton Museum*

The horn has been removed from its mount inboard of the right headlight, and the .30-caliber machine gun is not installed. The vehicle number, B-12, is stenciled on the muzzle covers of the three recoilless rifles to the right but not on the covers for the other ones. *Patton Museum*

An Ontos crew of the 1st Marine Division, Fleet Marine Force, practices coming ashore from a landing craft at the beach at Camp Pendleton on May 25, 1964. Faintly visitble at the rear of the hull is the registration number, 226870. *USMC*

Ontos drivers were under instructions to drive the vehicle slowly from a landing-craft ramp into the water and to proceed at a moderate speed until landing, to avoid creating a bow wave. A deepwater-fording kit had to be installed for water deeper than 24 inches. *USMC*

Three Ontos from Battalion Landing Team 2, 6th Marines, conduct live-firing exercises across a bay during a training deployment to Porto Scudo, Sardinia, in 1966. Packing tubes for 106 mm ammunition are lying next to the vehicles, and the recoilless rifles are kicking up a great deal of dust. *Naval History and Heritage Command*

A Marine M50A1 comes ashore in southern Thailand during Operation Jungle Drum III on March 20, 1965. This was a joint US-Thai exercise to develop cooperative counterinsurgency methods. An extra 5-gallon liquid container is lashed to the hull forward of the stock 5-gallon container. *Naval History and Heritage Command*

Among the first USMC armor to land in the Republic of Vietnam on March 8, 1965, was the 3rd Platoon, Company C, 3rd Antitank Battalion. An M50A1 of that unit exits a landing craft on Red Beach II at Đà Nang. The vehicle number is painted on the right fender, and the insignia of the 3rd Marine Division is on the left fender. *National Archives*

An Ontos takes up position on the beachhead at Đà Nang during the March 1965 landings. By the end of that year, there would be approximately sixty-five Ontos in country. Although the Ontos would see its first real combat a month later in the Dominican Republic, this strange little vehicle was about to make its debut in sustained combat in Vietnam. *National Archives*

On April 10, 1965, a Marine Ontos of the 3rd Antitank Battalion rolls along Red Beach at Đà Nang. Protracted operation on sand would quickly wear out the tracks: in particular, the sand would wear down the heads of the track bolts to the point that they could not be removed without great effort. *National Archives*

A column of vehicles of the 9th Marine Expeditionary Brigade, including at least two M50s, is proceeding across a beach at Đà Nang in March 1965. Gear is heaped on the glacis of the lead Ontos, including camouflage netting and a section of spare track. *National Archives*

An Ontos of the 3rd Marine Division drives off a landing craft at Red Beach, Đà Nang, on April 10, 1965, while members of a beach party look on. The upper part of another Ontos is visible on the second landing craft. *National Archives*

Two M50s are coming ashore at Chu Lai, Republic of Vietnam, on May 7, 1965. They were assigned to the 3rd Marine Division. A long section of spare track is draped over the right side of the glacis of the closer vehicle, and a bedroll and a combat pack are strapped to the recoilless-rifle barrels.

During civil disturbances in the Dominican Republic in the spring of 1965, the 6th Marine Expeditionary Unit, including an Ontos company, was dispatched to evacuate US civilians and defend the American embassy. There the Ontos saw its first combat. This Ontos is patrolling a street in Santo Domingo in early May. *Naval History and Heritage Command*

A Marine Ontos crew seeks a defensive position upon landing on the beach at Chu Lai in June 1965. A rations box is stowed on the front of the vehicle, and a folding cot is hanging from the side. Stuffed in between two of the recoilless rifles is a bedroll. An extra 5-gallon liquid container is secured to the side of the hull, and several M1 helmets with camouflage covers are stowed on the vehicle. Masking tape has been applied to the fronts of the two headlights. In the background is an LVTP-5 amphibious personnel carrier. *Naval History and Heritage Command*

Members of the 7th Marine Regiment, 3rd Marine Division, are taking a chow break in a command-post area during Operation Starlight, in the Republic of Vietnam, on August 19, 1965. Two M50s are parked on the other side of the trees. The closer one has a tailpipe extension on the rear of the muffler, part of a deepwater-fording kit. *National Archives*

During Operation Black Snake in the Republic of Vietnam on November 1, 1965, an Ontos is standing guard in a field while Marine infantrymen advance through an adjacent rice paddy. The vehicle was assigned to Company K of an unidentified regiment of the 3rd Marine Division. "USMC" and the registration number "226889" are stenciled in yellow on the rear part of the sponson. *National Archives*

Two Ontos are being transported on the deck of the tank-landing ship USS *Henry County* (LST-825) during Operation Jack Stay, an amphibious operation in the Rừng Sát Special Zone some 20 miles southeast of Saigon in March–April 1966. The vehicles are clear of the extra gear often stowed on Ontos during amphibious operations. *Naval History and Heritage Command*

The crew of one of the Ontos being transported on USS *Henry County* during Operation Jack Stay is manning the vehicle, evidently checking out its systems and observing the shoreline. Interestingly, the Ontos does not appear to be secured to the deck of the landing craft. *Naval History and Heritage Command*

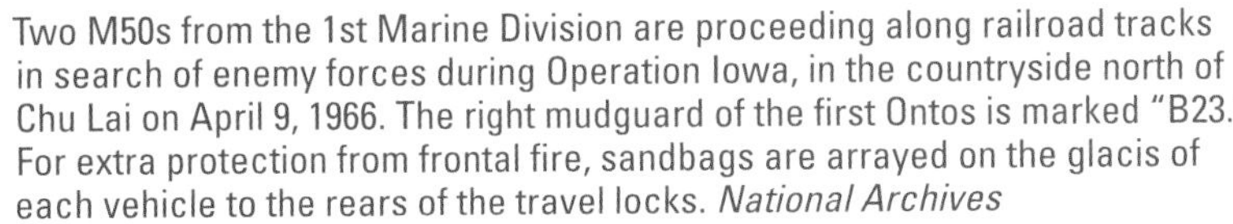

Two M50s from the 1st Marine Division are proceeding along railroad tracks in search of enemy forces during Operation Iowa, in the countryside north of Chu Lai on April 9, 1966. The right mudguard of the first Ontos is marked "B23." For extra protection from frontal fire, sandbags are arrayed on the glacis of each vehicle to the rears of the travel locks. *National Archives*

Having completed nighttime perimeter defense, the crew of an Ontos from A Company, 1st Antitank Battalion, 1st Marine Division, are proceeding through coastal sand dunes away from their post shortly after dawn on May 28, 1966. This was during Operation Mobile. A toolbox with a peaked top is stashed behind the left headlight array. *National Archives*

A Marine Ontos is advancing past sand dunes near a beach in the Republic of Vietnam in May 1966. "C 12" is painted in large figures on the rear doors. The elbow-shaped tailpipe is missing from the rear of the muffler.

An M274A5 "Mule" with a 106 mm recoilless rifle mounted on it, *center*, and an M50 Ontos, *right*, have taken up position in a valley 15 miles north of Hué and Phú Bài during Operation Cherokee, on May 8, 1966. A tailpipe extension for deepwater fording is visible above the rear of the superstructure of the Ontos. *National Archives*

The crewmen of an Ontos positioned behind concertina wire are vigilant while performing watch duty at Chu Lai during Operation Mobile on May 28, 1966. *National Archives*

In a final photo taken at Chu Lai during Operation Mobile on May 28, 1966, an Ontos is moving out to provide fire support for Marine infantrymen. *National Archives*

In a photo that likely shows the same Ontos and crew as in the preceding photo, a Marine is loading a round into the chamber of the upper-right recoilless rifle, on the perimeter of the base at Chu Lai on May 28, 1966. A flash suppressor is on the muzzle of the M1919 .30-caliber machine gun on the turret. *National Archives*

An Ontos with improvised additional sandbag armor moves out to accompany the 1st and 2nd Battalions, 7th Marines, in Quang Ngai Province in June 1966. *USMC Archives and Special Collections*

Several M50s from the 1st Marine Division are lined up just before the start of an offensive, code-named Operation Incinerator, on June 1, 1966. Three M50s and four tanks, including the M48 in the right background, participated in this attack. On the nearest Ontos, there is an expanded steel sleeve over the exhaust pipe, in addition to an expanded steel shield over the muffler. *National Archives*

This M50A1 of Company A, 1st Antitank Battalion, was photographed in 1966. On the front left fender is a profile of a pig with "BACON" written above it, perhaps an allusion to the Ontos' nickname, "Pig." The recoilless-rifle travel locks appear to be missing their C-shaped top clamps, and rubber shock cords with S hooks have been substituted as an expedient. The extra 5-gallon liquid container on the side of the hull is marked "OIL" on its side, and a conical flash suppressor is affixed to the .30-caliber machine gun barrel. The louvered engine-access and transmission-access doors, characteristic of the M50A1, are in evidence, and visible on the glacis to the front of the driver's hatch is the actuating rod for the travel lock, which the driver could raise and lower from within the vehicle. *Patton Museum*

A column of Ontos supporting Marine infantrymen pause for a break in the middle of a rice paddy during a mission near Phú Bài. The lead vehicle has three extra 5-gallon liquid containers stowed on the glacis. The horn is missing from its socket next to the right headlight; this item was often not installed on the Ontos. The vehicle number is painted on the right mudguard, the A standing for Company A. With its low ground pressure, the Ontos could often operate in muddy terrain where tanks would get bogged down. The tracks of the second Ontos in the column have not sunk much farther into the mud than the ankles of the adjacent Marines. *Patton Museum*

An M50A1 of 1st Platoon, Company C, 1st Antitank Battalion, crashes through brush during Operation Mobile near Chu Lai in May 1966. The vehicle number, C-11, is stenciled on the crewmen's CVC helmets, and the driver and commander/gunner are wearing M1955 flak vests. The clamps of the travel lock have been released from over the barrels of the recoilless rifles so the lock can be lowered quickly and the rifles put into play if a target presents itself. A spare section of track is carried on front of the vehicle. These sections were 60 inches long by 20 inches wide, and five of them were spliced together to make a track assembly. Supplies of tracks in country were running low by 1966, so Ontos crews took pains to carry at least one section of spare track into the field. *Patton Museum*

Even though the frontal armor of the Ontos was well sloped to deflect small-arms fire and shrapnel, the ½ inch of steel offered notoriously poor protection against anything larger. Thus, the crew of this Ontos operating in Vietnam during Operation Iowa has piled sandbags on the glacis to offer an additional buffer against enemy fire. It is unclear if the panels added to the lower sides of the upper hull acted as retainers for more sandbags or as racks for extra equipment. The vehicle number is stenciled on the front face of each of the muzzle covers but is illegible. Long straps are attached to these covers to tie them in place. Finally, local camouflage has been arranged around the vehicle. *Patton Museum*

An Ontos has taken up position in a field in Vietnam, with an M48A3 Patton medium tank standing nearby. A close inspection shows that numerous extra stores, including liquid containers, cartons, helmets, and other gear, are stowed on the Ontos' hull, and the rear doors are open. The breech ends of the recoilless rifles are wrapped with a light-colored material, possibly makeshift covers instead of the standard-issue Olive Drab canvas covers. During the US involvement in Vietnam, few enemy armored vehicles presented themselves, so American tank and antitank vehicles such as the M48 and Ontos were generally relegated to roles for which they had not been designed, such as fire support and reconnaissance. Interestingly, virtually all Ontos officers were infantrymen, although battalion commanders were armor specialists. *Patton Museum*

In support of Operation County Fair in February 1966, unit mechanics from A Company, 3rd Antitank Battalion, fitted this M50A1 Ontos with an 18-inch Crouse-Hinds searchlight for use in nighttime perimeter defense to aid nighttime firing. The support brackets are attached to the .30-caliber machine gun cross-arm so that the searchlight can traverse with the turret. Elevation orientation is done manually by the crew. These searchlights had previously been mounted on tanks but became surplus when the tanks were equipped with infrared-capable Xenon searchlights. *National Archives*

In a base camp on Hill 41 south of Huế, an Ontos has been positioned in a sandbagged emplacement to provide perimeter defense. During June 1966, a section of Ontos of Company A, 3rd Antitank Battalion, is known to have been deployed to Hill 41. Firing beehive antipersonnel ammunition packed with hundreds of flechettes, the Ontos could have a devastating effect on attacking troops. *Patton Museum*

An Ontos from 2nd Platoon, C Company, 3rd Marine Antitank Battalion, is advancing toward a battle on September 20, 1966. Smoke from the fight is in the left background. Marine troops were driving Vietcong forces toward the Ontos. Dustcovers are still on the muzzles and the breeches of the recoilless rifles. *National Archives*

A convoy proceeding from Chu Lai to Đà Nẵng, including an M50 Ontos from the 1st Marine Division, passes through a Vietnamese village on December 18, 1966. Although difficult to discern, the number "1322" is painted in large figures on the right mudguard. *National Archives*

In a photo related to the preceding one, an Ontos from 2nd Platoon, C Company, 3rd Marine Antitank Battalion, is firing one of its 106 mm recoilless rifles at a suspected enemy position during a sweep on September 20, 1966. The firing of the piece generated considerable smoke and dust, temporarily obscuring the gunner's view. *National Archives*

Pfc. Ramos Rodriguez, USMC, from 2nd Platoon, A Company, 3rd Amphibious Tractor Battalion, is cleaning the breechblock of the lower 106 mm recoilless rifle on the left side of an M50 Ontos. He is grasping the operating lever for the breechblock. The photo was taken in Vietnam during 1966. *National Archives*

A loader inserts a 106 mm round into the breech while another crewman looks on. The steel casings of the ammunition were varnished to prevent rust and were perforated to allow some of the gas to vent to the rear when the weapon was fired, thus equalizing the forward force of the propellant and projectile and canceling the recoil forces. *Patton Museum*

An observer is standing by as an Ontos fires at a suspected enemy position in the Republic of Vietnam sometime in 1966. The vehicle was serving with the 3rd Marine Division. "A 21" is painted in yellow on the rear doors; the registration number, also in yellow, is 226870. *National Archives*

An M50 Ontos marked "B 22" on the rear is advancing along an abandoned railroad grade in support of C Company, 1st Battalion, 4th Marine Regiment, during Operation Deckhouse IV on February 17, 1967. A motto, "[two illegible words] SILENCE," is stenciled on the turret hatch door. *National Archives*

This M50 from the 3rd Marine Division, employed in the defense of Camp Evans in the Republic of Vietnam, was photographed on June 27, 1967. A spare-track section is lying across the front of the glacis, and a 5-gallon liquid container is strapped to the superstructure, while the holder for a liquid container is empty. National Archives

The crew of an M50 Ontos takes a break before moving into a position at Con Thien, Republic of Vietnam, on October 2, 1967. For personal protection, the crewmen are wearing M1 steel helmets with camouflage covers and M55 flak vests. *National Archives*

An Ontos with "A 34" roughly painted in yellow on the rear is positioned behind sandbags as it guards the perimeter of the Khe Sahn Combat Base on October 23, 1967. A section of spare track is lying against the superstructure above the muffler. Three months later, Khe Sanh would be the scene of a fierce, months-long siege and battle. *National Archives*

The three members of the crew of an M50 Ontos of the 1st Marine Division are cleaning the vehicle after it got muddy during recent heavy rains, somewhere in Vietnam on November 3, 1967. The letter A is on the left rear door, and the registration number, 226751, is to the rear of the muffler. *National Archives*

The marking "C-5-2" in yellow is on the right mudguard of this Ontos, as crewmen reload the recoilless rifles alongside a sandbagged ammunition bunker at Con Thien on November 25, 1967. *National Archives*

Two members of an Ontos crew are loading rounds into the 106 mm recoilless rifles in the Company B area at the 1st Marine Division base at Con Thien, Republic of Vietnam, on November 22, 1967. Photos indicate that when the spotting rifles were not in use, they were protected by covers as seen here. *National Archives*

The loader is peering at the camera through the open breech of the lower-right recoilless rifle of this Ontos. *National Archives*

An M50A1 Ontos, marked "B 12," is positioned for perimeter defense at an unidentified base of the 1st Marine Division in Vietnam in 1967. The .50-caliber spotting rifles are in view above the upper recoilless-rifle barrels. *National Archives*

The same M50A1 portrayed in the preceding photo is viewed from the left front while on perimeter-defense duty. The registration number, 226787, is faintly visible near the rear of the superstructure. Because the antennas are mounted on the rear of the turret of this Ontos, rather than on the rear of the hull, we know this vehicle is equipped with a solid-state AN/VRC-12 radio. *National Archives*

In another photo of the M50A1 marked "B 12," a crewman is preparing to load a round into one of the 106 mm recoilless rifles. On the left mudguard is a yellow bridge classification sign with the numeral 9 on it. *National Archives*

An M50 Ontos is positioned to face to the west of Observation Post No. 1 at Nui Con Thien, Republic of Vietnam, on February 3, 1968. The rear doors are marked "A 15." Original documentation with the photo suggests that the vehicle was operating in support of F Company, 2/1st Marines. *National Archives*

An Ontos from the 3rd Marine Division is positioned behind a masonry wall during the Battle of Huế on February 11, 1968. A tailpipe extension, part of a deepwater-fording kit, is attached to the rear of the muffler. *National Archives*

An Ontos leads commandeered vehicles during the Battle for Huế City, 1968. The Ontos is spearheading the effort to medevac and resupply Marines. *USMC*

During the Battle of Huế City, an Ontos fires on an enemy sniper position. During the battle the Ontos crews used HEAT rounds to penetrate heavy masonry structures, and APERS-T rounds against infantry, along with firing the rounds into masonry to create a dust cloud to allow Marine infantry to advance under cover. *USMC Archives and Special Collections*

An exhausted Marine crewman takes a nap on the glacis of his Ontos during the Battle of Hué on February 23, 1968. This gives a clear view of the brackets that held the headlights; the right brush guard is missing. *National Archives*

An Ontos driver wearing an M1 steel helmet is looking out of his hatch as the vehicle makes its way through a Vietnamese village in February 1968. A bridge-classification sign with the number "9" is on the right mudguard. On the left side of the superstructure, with a hose wrapped around it, is a track jack, an implement used to draw the track together when it was being repaired. *National Archives*

An M50 Ontos from G Company, 2nd Battalion, 3rd Marine Regiment, is departing from the Marine base at Cam Lo, Republic of Vietnam, on November 21, 1968. Although the long section of spare track on the glacis would be essential if the vehicle struck (and survived) a mine, repairing the unique tracks of the Ontos was a very difficult task under the best of conditions. *National Archives*

Members of a Marine Ontos are repairing a right track on their vehicle at a base in Vietnam sometime in 1968. The left track also was under repair, since a track jack is clamped to that track, to the immediate rear of the 5-gallon liquid container. The left track of the Ontos to the far left is also under repair and is laid out to the front of the chassis. *National Archives*

Ontos were used for perimeter defense during the siege of Khe Sahn. This March 29, 1968, photo of Onto 17C illustrates how the vehicles were dug in during this action. William W. *Legal Collection, Marine Corps History Division*

An M50 Ontos marked "A34" on the right mudguard shows extensive rust at the USMC ordnance shop at Dong Ha in 1968. The following year, the Marines transferred their remaining M50s in Vietnam to the US Army, where the vehicles continued in service in dwindling numbers, as damaged vehicles were cannibalized to keep others operational. By 1970, the Ontos had been retired from service in Vietnam. *National Archives*

Marine Corps M50s awaiting repairs are lined up at the ordnance shop at Dong Ha, Republic of Vietnam, in 1968. The vehicles and the recoilless rifles exhibit a considerable amount of rust, which could quickly overtake a vehicle in the humid climate of Southeast Asia. Dong Ha is on the coast of the South China Sea, and the salt air accelerated the corrosion of metals. *National Archives*

In March 1969, a deception plan enabled the insertion of two Ontos into the area southwest of Khe Sanh during Operation Maine Crag. The Ontos were stripped of all superficial armor and the recoilless rifles. Plywood "blades" disguised the vehicles as bulldozers. The two Ontos were inserted by CH-54; the recoilless rifles and personnel were inserted by CH-46 from Vandegrift Combat Base. *USMC*

Seen on June 10, 1969, at Hill 10, the home of the 1st Battalion, 7th Marines, this Ontos is very near the end of its service life. An ongoing shortage of repair parts, especially tracks, made maintaining the heavily used vehicles a challenge. As the Marines began leaving Vietnam, many of these vehicles were turned over to the Army rather than being shipped back stateside. When no longer operable, the Army used them as stationary bunkers. *Kenneth W. Koldys Collection, Marine Corps History Division*